Steve

# WALK-ON U™

## THE SHOCKING TRUTH BEHIND FOOTBALL'S UNSUNG UNDERDOGS

"Make a Statement!"

TIM LAVIN

WALK-ON U™

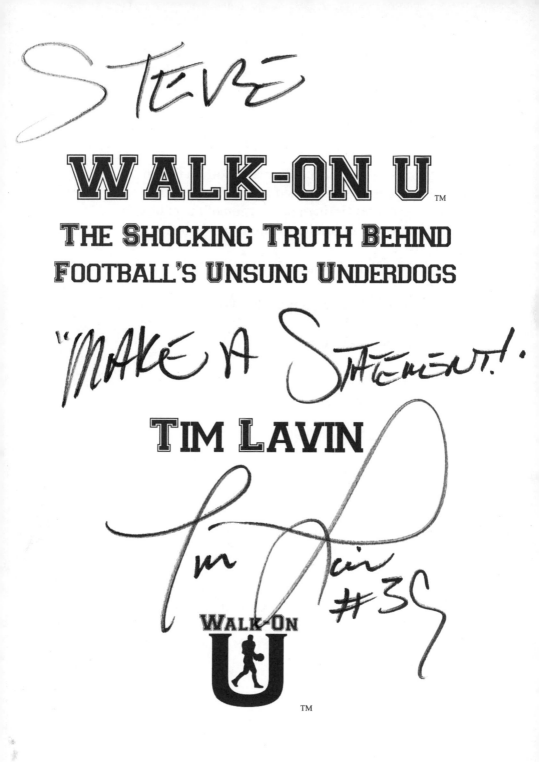

Printed in the United States of America

First Paperback Printing, September 2013

ISBN 978-0-9897721-0-5

Walk-On U, LLC
412 Olive Avenue
No. 560
Huntington Beach, CA 92648

www.Walk-OnU.com

Cover Photograph by Jay Lavin

Design by Tim Lavin

Graphics and Layout by Danny Griffith, Amanda Althoff

Inside Photos: Associated Press (AP Images), Bill Emerson, Tim Lavin.

Inside Photos Layout: Suzanne Lavin

# Dedication

I dedicate this book to my parents, Ed and Derreth Lavin. Every good thing I have done in my life is in direct relation to their teaching, advice, support and love. Every stupid thing I have ever done in my life is because I did not listen to my parents!

Mom and Dad,

I love you more than anything and THANK YOU for EVERYTHING!

Your third son,

*Timothy*

# TABLE OF CONTENTS

# FOREWORD

## by Jim Walsh

In February 1988, I made the decision to leave the formal coaching ranks as running game coordinator at Stanford University to start a much needed life management program for athletes, their parents, and coaches. Since then, I have worked with thousands of people throughout the nation. The purpose of the program was to prepare participants—regardless of their level of involvement—to ensure their physical and mental well-being. For years, sports pages have chronicled the mishaps of celebrity athletes. They all have similar stories of being blessed with athletic prowess but cursed with celebrity fame, fortune, and the privilege that comes with it.

I was determined to show the world that there is another side of the story where young athletes, their families, and coaches have achieved great things both on and off the field. I have experienced first-hand every level of athletic participation and have met so many great people who have wonderful stories documenting their achievements.

One of the leading misconceptions concerning the athletic process is related to college recruiting. I experienced the highs and lows of this process both in my high school years and finally, after many setbacks, when I was awarded a scholarship at San Jose State University. My time spent with teammates both at college and professional levels showed me how many players had similar experiences and were misevaluated by the so-called "major colleges." I always was fascinated by the labeling that still occurs today regarding what is or isn't a D-I guy.

To see athletes like Steve Largent, Jerry Rice, and so many others who played at relatively small colleges go on to achieve Hall-of-Fame stature was amazing. What these players, and so many like them, had was an abundance of talent and an over-abundance of what it takes to compete at the highest level for so many years! Trust me; it isn't easy, even though many of these elite players make it look effortless at times. Their hard work, sacrifice, and commitment are often overlooked due to their superior athletic skills and amazing accomplishments on the field.

The other end of the athletic spectrum includes so many talented athletes with certain limitations, height, weight, speed, and or labels assigned to them that put them in categories such as "over-achievers," "good practice guys," or "walk-ons." Those are the rare souls who, against the odds, achieve greatness despite criticism and labels assigned to them by coaches and peers. The achievers never accept those labels and overcome whatever challenges are set before them simply for the love of the game and because of a deep inner belief that they too can play this game and compete at a higher level.

For some, the rewards will never include game time, recognition by anyone outside the locker room, or compensation in the form of an athletic scholarship. The rewards they do receive; however—self-confidence, competitiveness, and ability to take direction as part of a team—remain constant companions throughout their lives. The respect they earn from peers, coaches, and those who understand their contribution is priceless. It transcends any scoreboard or accolade. When a player at the far end of the athletic spectrum receives team affirmation after a practice or scrimmage, it ignites an inner flame to continue the journey that many others won't complete.

I first met Tim Lavin while I was speaking at his former high school, Chaminade College Prep of West Hills, Calif. In the crowd, I could feel my message was being well received. I also could sense that one person in particular was on the edge of his seat and had an extraordinary intensity. I have seen this look before on the faces of competitors ready to take the necessary step that so many athletes talk about—but few actually do.

Tim Lavin had just completed his freshman year as a walk-on at USC and had come to hear me speak to the participants in the football program of his alma mater. Afterwards, I learned that even though Tim was named CIF Player of the Year, finishing second in

Southern California in rushing and scoring behind Russell White, one of the nation's top recruits, Tim received no scholarship offers. I had seen tape on White when I was coaching at Stanford. But after seeing Tim's tape for the first time, I was impressed with his size, vision, and yards gained when the line of scrimmage was not available. He made yards on his own! Tim told me USC granted him a walk-on opportunity.

For all high school players entering college football, the transition is difficult. The speed of the game intensifies, the comfort of a high school system is replaced by a new set of norms, vocabulary, pace, and the presence of seasoned players—ones who have been in the program for several years. I wanted to make certain that whatever the physical tests were for USC football that Tim Lavin's evaluation by the coaching staff upon entering his second year of training camp would be positive. In fact, due to Tim's intense focus, I wanted the coaches to be utterly amazed. Tim achieved that and more.

Tim went to practice every day not to make the team but to prove a point: He wanted to show he could play at this level! Every day was game day for Tim, but he knew that some of his teammates might resent his relentless efforts. His passion was unquestionable, and I loved to remind him that he was playing every day against the best defense in the nation. I told him the time would come when the defensive players would change their tune from, “Hey man, tone it down!” to “This guy is a stud!” He would then be ready for the biggest test yet; coaches recognizing he was for real. Tim transitioned from "just a walk-on" to his nickname of “Mad Dog” and became a force with which to be reckoned.

Tim was one of the most inspiring young athletes I ever coached and mentored. He knew the scholarship players would be given every opportunity, and that he would be forced to spend one or two years on the scout team, a mission with little status and even fewer rewards. Repeatedly, Tim was named Scout Team Player of the Week so often that they could no longer justify giving him the award. Still, Tim remained on the sidelines during games, suited up but never playing.

Frankly, most young players would have thrown up their hands, growing weary of feeling more like a tackling dummy than an athlete. But Tim remained confident, endured the drudgery, and kept a strong vision of his ultimate goal of playing on Saturday afternoon for USC. Tim persevered, proved his worthiness, and the coaches acknowledged his effort and talents by awarding him a scholarship, a place on the travel squad, and significant playing time on special teams and at his fullback position. His game day efforts as a Trojan ultimately garnered Tim two NFL tryouts, a far cry from his original walk-on status.

In the following pages, you will learn that Tim had guidance from people like me, others whom he could trust, as well as the support of his family. But no one could do for Tim what Tim needed to do for himself. I believe this is the greatest lesson you can learn. Life will present us with obstacles; challenges, even difficulties, but our responses to these realities are what determine our path as we become defined either as a victim, a survivor, or a conqueror!

I was able to assist Tim at critical times because I had been on the same road and was determined to make sure others would not have to experience what I went through. I thank God for the trials He presented me with and the blessings received when reaching the other side of those trials. After reading Tim's story, I am certain you will be encouraged, even inspired and ready to take on the next challenge in your life as a conqueror. Here's hoping you enjoy every step of the journey.

Jim Walsh

**About Jim Walsh**

Jim Walsh is a former college and NFL player, college and professional coach, President and Founder of A STEP BEYOND Training Systems, published author, Everything You Need to Know About College Sports Recruiting: A Guide for Players and Parents (Andrews McMeel Publishing, 1996), and C-level executive. He has dedicated his life to helping athletes on and off the field and is a national keynote speaker for athletic organizations, schools, colleges, universities, and businesses.

# INTRODUCTION

The biggest underdog in all of college sports is the "Walk-On." The term represents a stigma, a disgrace known only to those of us who have donned the shoes worn by the very few. Those who have been there can attest to the shocking stories. But, truly understanding the experience in its entirety often becomes impossible to comprehend by the uninitiated. The erratic and perplexing school decisions and unconscionable NCAA rules all lead to a torrent of rollercoaster emotions on the part of walk-on players. Walk-ons are counted here, but not over there. They are needed but ignored, valued but scorned, encouraged but held back.

So many walk-on players are game-day capable yet forced to endlessly climb a mountain to prove their worthiness. Yet no matter how far they ascend, the top mountain always eludes them. As the climb appears to get shorter, the walk-on player often gets pushed further down the mountain for reasons that are never clear. Changes become setbacks, and nothing but cloudy explanations survive.

To the crowd, walk-ons are just hard workers with big hearts. But, to a Walk-On Impact Player, there's a much larger scenario in play. The odds are against him, but pursuing the path of least resistance is not in his DNA. Walk-ons are not regular people.

They have higher expectations than average. They battle long and hard and end up with physical and emotional scars to prove it. The struggles seem endless, but walk-ons remain tireless. An inner determination that they won't let others shape their world catapults them to challenge the norm, push past set standards to create their own. It's a whole different world, and few realize they're in it and no one knows what they're experiencing. I'm going to take you inside that world.

At some point, crippling pain and miserable heartache take a back seat to hope and optimism. As the journey continues, those relentless enough to pursue their dream can break through the wall and see their dream shine through. The physical, mental, and emotional journey that "game-day capable" walk-ons endure is unlike anything you have ever heard before. These experiences will shock, amaze, and bewilder you.

There will be critics of what we expose here, but I am certain that none of the critics have ever been walk-ons. In the end, a new realization will prevail. A relentlessly shamed group of wannabe star athletes will emerge with greater respect, enhanced relevance, and significantly more pride. Hopefully, change will take shape in the minds of the NCAA decision makers and new rules will evolve for tomorrow's walk-ons. The "way it is" needs to become the "way it was." *Us and them* must come together as one, which is the way it should be.

In seeking guidance while writing this book, I had many discussions with industry professionals. They all concluded that this story would be revolutionary and give rise to a massive exposure of unfair practices in the college sports world. They all assumed I was going to hire a writer, or a ghost writer, or a co-author. I said no.

The challenge - and responsibility - of shining a light on the plight of walk-ons must be told by someone who has lived in that world. It must be told with passion and integrity to bring the walk-ons' stories to life so as to educate a nation. People should feel and experience the disgrace and humiliation. They need to see the dark funnel cloud of twisted and humbling travels undertaken in search of a victory that will not be displayed on a college scoreboard. As the shattered hopes and dreams of former star players finally mend together from sheer grit, a private jubilee begins to emerge that can only be experienced by a party of one: the lone walk-on.

It is my job to take this extraordinary experience and transform it into a story that describes the incredible journey of a unique breed of individuals. These players, right out of high school, experience a lifetime of emotions during just a few short years. I will reveal the unwritten rules behind the rules and show you how they are sometimes broken. It is all part of the underground world of college football and its unsung underdogs, the walk-ons.

I am very proud of my uncommon journey. My name is Tim Lavin and I'm a Walk-On.

***

# Chapter 1
# The Truth

This was very hard for me to write as I struggled with telling the whole walk-on story from top to bottom. I was concerned some people might have their feelings hurt. However, after scores of people gave me advice, I decided just to tell the whole story. As they say, the truth will set you free.

When I originally wrote this story, I told the truth about what happened, but I changed the names of key people and created a fictitious school name. I did that to protect people's feelings, and I didn't want certain individuals to think I was a bitter ex-athlete with an axe to grind. Nor did I want to spark a confrontation with anyone associated with my beloved university, the University of Southern California.

Over the past few years of this book's writing, I sought advice from dozens of advisers and consulted with as many people as I could who were well respected in the USC community, the book publishing world, and the media whom I had hoped would help get the book's message out to the public. I learned that a book filled with made-up names and pretend universities would most likely lead down a path of disinterested readers. Nor would it stimulate much discussion, even though the book was based on the truth. The book would struggle with success if the media couldn't ask me questions such as "what happened when…" or "how did that make you feel after…."

If I were tight lipped in order to protect a few people's feelings, then I would not be considered for a serious interview nor would I be standing up for what I truly believed in—that walk-ons deserve better. In the end, I rewrote this story using all of the actual names, and I hope people read the entire book to completely understand how I truly feel. I do believe that the truth will set us free.

**The Beginning**

I was a high school running back who fortunately earned many awards over many exciting Friday nights, but I had only one goal, earning a football scholarship at a Division I college. I wanted to play on Saturdays. That sought-after goal would not be realized after graduation. However, I was recruited and then invited by USC to pay full tuition, and come out to practice with the team, joining a small cadre of fellow walk-ons. Walk-ons filled out the ranks of big time college football; they played the positions, and ran the plays each week of the team's opponents. In practice during the week before games the starting offense and starting defense would practice against the 3rd, 4th, and 5th string players, swelling with walk-ons, and called, the scout team.

In year two of my tenure at USC, I was making waves on scout team and pushing for playing time on special teams. I was just a redshirt freshman walk-on, but Coach Bobby April loved my intensity and started flirting with putting me on second-string punt block, kickoff, and kickoff return teams. However, I just could not break onto the travel squad roster even though I was listed as a backup on three special teams. If a guy got hurt and we were playing at home, I would go in. But if the team was on the road, and I wasn't there, somebody else would be the backup.

Determined to play on Saturdays, I felt I had earned the opportunity not only to travel and contribute on game day, but to get a scholarship. At this point, I was starting to figure out the game—not the game of football—but the political game of "scholarship players versus walk-ons." As players, we called it: "***The System***."

I came to realize that my style of play would eventually get me noticed, that I would climb the ladder of respect, and even get my name thrown high up on the depth chart. But the countervailing influence, when it really came down to it, was that walk-ons (aside from kickers) never make the travel squad and are an absolute last resort on game day.

All through the season, I remained on scout team and practiced against one of the top defenses in the country. I was routinely told by my teammates that I was hated and feared—a true compliment for a scout team player. I fought with defensive players every day when we scrimmaged because I was going all out and making it difficult on the defense. Many of these respected players went on to have long NFL careers.

Junior Seau, one of the best linebackers ever to play the game, and a 20-year NFL veteran, would often have words with me. Usually in passing he would hit me and say something like, "Ease up a little out there today, Mad Dog." But one day, after a long, hot, grueling practice in which Seau and I got into an all-out punching brawl, he stopped by my locker afterwards, reached out to shake my hand and said, "Mad Dog, I love it! Don't stop. Don't stop! You belong at the other end."

The starting offense practiced at the south end of the field while the starting defense at the north end. It is the goal of every scout team player, regardless of whether you are a scholarship player or a walk-on, to graduate from the practice squad and move to the other end of the field. If you are an offensive player, you want to be at the offensive end of the field because that means you are among the top two or three at your position on the team's depth chart. But if you are at the other end of the field, that means you are listed fourth or lower on the depth chart and relegated to scout team. Seau knew how hard I was working to get to the "other end" of the field. He felt I deserved being among the top three at fullback, and of course so did I.

Another Trojan great, safety Mark Carrier, was part of the defense that loved to go after me. Carrier won the Jim Thorpe Award, which is presented to the best defensive back in the country. He then went on to have an 11-year NFL career. Of course at the time, we were practicing on the same team, and I had no idea what he would do in the NFL. I did know, however, that he was considered one of the best at his position, and I had the privilege of going up against him every day.

I remember stirring up a lot of commotion one scrimmage and getting the best of the defense. I was so keen on getting noticed and making a statement in front of the coaches that I may have inadvertently said a few things out loud in order to stir up the pot. During one play, I carried the ball up the middle for about nine yards. The defensive coaches went ballistic that they couldn't stop the scout team. I was having punches thrown at me at the bottom of the pile. When I rose to my feet, I let the coaches know that their defensive team was getting run over by a scout team full of walk-ons! That didn't go over so well.

D-Line Coach Kevin Wolthausen unleashed a tirade of expletives on me as I went back to the huddle. Then he went to the defensive huddle and screamed at his linemen. On the very next play, all 11 defenders ran at me to take me down. I am not sure if the coach ordered “the hit” on me or if the players decided that on their own after the coach walked away. But as I set up to block on the next play with all 11 players charging and tackling me, our scout team threw a pass. With no defensive backs because they were all dog piling on me, our walk-on wide receiver, Tom Brown, caught the ball and scored a touchdown. When the 11 players were pulled from my flattened body, I realized we had scored. I got up and started singing the Notre Dame Victory March fight song. They hated me at that moment, and it was exhilarating!

On some days, we had weight lifting after football practice. This was one of them, and Mark Carrier approached me in the weight room. I was off in the corner lifting by myself. Again, respecting Mark for being one of the best players in the country, I felt rewarded that he sought me out and said something to me.

He shouted “MAD DOG!” at me and then started barking like a dog. It was funny, but I didn't crack a smile. Still focused and intense from the all-out dog pile during practice 30 minutes earlier, I stared back at him stone-faced.

“You are one tough son of a bitch,” Carrier said.

I jumped up from the bench and asked him a question: “Mark, do you think I am good enough to be at the other end of the field?” His answer set the tone for my next move and the chapter *The Promise.*

“Hell yes, Lavin, but, you’re a victim of the system,” and he walked away. I knew exactly what he meant.

***

# Chapter 2

# Practice Walk-On VS. Game-Day Walk-On

Coaches love walk-ons. They need them. Without walk-ons teams would be forced to prepare completely differently from how they do now—much more like the NFL game. Having no walk-ons would alter the college game.

The mindsets of *practice walk-ons* and *game-day walk-ons* are vastly different. Some similarities do exist, however. Both attend the college or university without the help of an athletic scholarship. Both will be put at the bottom of the depth chart behind all the scholarship players.

Collectively, walk-ons make up about 20 to 25 players on your average Division I football team out of the 105 to 110 players. Normally, 85 players are on scholarship. Playing on Saturday is the ultimate goal. Some do, most don't. Those who don't, typically fall into the practice-walk-on category. Those who do play are an entirely different breed and have an enormously different walk-on experience. Those are the ga*me-day walk-ons*.

Practice walk-ons normally go to their favorite school. It may be the school their parents or another family member went to. They might have grown up dreaming of being part of that specific institution's program. They probably have had their heart set on it as far back as they can remember. Or it may be the school to which they were academically accepted. Regardless, they will be content to have made the team and just be happy to be part of it. Their dedication to keep going, to practice and get crushed repeatedly, and keep coming back over and over again is more than admirable. They take brutal hits, suffer injuries, miss outside social activities, and spend scores of hours every week just to be part of the team. That is their payoff, just being part of the team.

The Practice Walk-On knows he is probably not good enough to play on Saturdays, and does not really expect to. Getting playing time during the last few moments of an already-decided game is the best they can hope for.

However, if you expect to be a Game-day Walk-On, fasten your seat belt for the ride of your life. You prepare physically and endure the mental and emotional rollercoaster en route to shock the system. It is the same system that will hold you down while trying to keep you in your place at the bottom of the ladder. However, staying down is not an option regardless of how many times you get stepped on, lied to, or pushed aside. You are not content being a practice player and will go above and beyond all things to prove you will supplant the scholarship players on your way to playing on Saturday.

You know, or quickly learn, that you are capable of playing on game day, but you also come to learn there are no plans for you to showcase your talents. You certainly are not known as a *game-day walk-on*—at least not yet. They have a different title for you. To the coaching staff, you are just a practice walk-on, someone they can use to help their recruited scholarship players get to the next level. You have to overcome the perception that this role is involuntarily imposed upon you. The glass ceiling is actually a concrete slab and you have four or five years to bust through it.

Many coaches suffer from the w*alk-on syndrome.* The walk-on syndrome is the philosophy that walk-ons are feeble human mannequins short on talent and used for the sole purpose of being blocking and tackling dummies in practice with no hope of ever being taken seriously as possible game-day contributors.

That mindset by stubborn, inflexible coaches hell-bent on proving themselves right will do everything in their power to keep you in your place so you won't have the opportunity to outshine their coveted recruit they spent years coddling. The recruiting process is a very big pamper-fest. Coaches will sweet-talk your family and tell you everything you want to hear to accept their scholarship offer. With so many other offers to consider, coaches wait on pins and needles for National High School Signing Day. And when that special student-athlete prospect has finally signed on the dotted line, the coach jumps for joy and holds a special celebration. Now, he has to keep his promise and make sure that young man who just signed those scholarship papers becomes the great player the coach told everyone he would become.

But wait. Practice starts and there is some no-name, good-for-nothing walk-on out there running around, knocking people to the ground, and creating havoc. Oh no! Suddenly Mr. Coach has an unexpected crisis on his hands.

The political game begins and the game-day walk-on is now knee-deep in the saga playing out on the gridiron. Knowing he should be moving up the ladder on the depth chart, he continuously fights, day-in and day-out suffering the demanding and harsh conditions of the scout team. It's a thankless job, and the punishment is dished out on both sides of the ball. The proof is there for everyone to see: The *Game-day Walk-On* is better than *Mr. Hollywood Recruit*! But, the coach is not budging. It's his pride that keeps him glued to his position. So, the backbreaking effort gets more heated.

All the unstoppable walk-ons are like newly-trained gladiators, having to prove themselves and dominate at their position in practice at a very high level putting the coach in a very compromising position. The walk-on essentially forces the coach to make decisions he never wanted to make. While watching film in the coach's-only meetings, another coach breaks the silence … a coach willing to speak the truth. Shining his red-dot laser beam at the video screen and right on the walk-on, he declares, "*This is your guy right here!*"

The game-day walk-on may have to wait years for that to happen. Unfortunately, the gut-wrenching wait may never end. And yet, the walk-on is out there every day, swinging the hammer, chipping away at the rock for it to crumble. The anxiety is merciless—a daily pit in the stomach. But giving up is not an option regardless of how ruthless the situation has become.

When the day ends, the *practice walk-on* heads back to the locker room for a shower and another day is in the books. Though battered and bruised, he'll probably whistle his way back to his apartment to study, watch TV, or perhaps meet up with friends.

Yet, the *game-day walk-on* is overcome with questions. Did I do enough today? Are they talking about me in coaches meetings? Will they give me an opportunity on special teams? What will they see on film tonight? Did I make any mistakes? Will they focus on the great plays I made today? Or will they be more concerned with what their scholarship players did wrong rather than what I did right?

These questions and the tension they produce place a stranglehold on your entire nervous system. TV, studying, or meeting with friends is the last thing on your mind. You have a job to accomplish, a coach to win over, and a game plan to make for the next day consisting of *what else can I do?*

While both sets of walk-ons are physically beat up from the demanding practice, it is a far different mental and emotional situation for the game-day walk-on. The mental anguish swirling around in your head is overwhelming. It breaks you emotionally, but you privately persevere, get stronger, and head back to attack it again the next day. Watching the game from the sidelines is totally unacceptable. There must be a way to prove you are an impact player and belong on that field come Saturday afternoon!

This book is about game-day walk-ons and the battles they face every day.

***

# Chapter 3
# The Promise

I fed off the compliments I received from my fellow teammates—Junior Seau, Mark Carrier and many other players—which only inspired me more. I came to the realization that something was going to break, and a tough decision needed to be made. I was *not* going to be a victim of "The System."

The System was, and still is, the entire political culture of college football, including the walk-on world. With regard to walk-ons, it was the unjust NCAA rules governing training table, the treatment received from anyone who thought you were less of a player because you had the moniker "walk-on" next to your name, the lack of opportunities to prove yourself, and the decisions that kept being made to keep you down just when you were climbing up the ladder. There are scores of examples nationwide from the unjust college sports world that continues to keep walk-ons from getting ahead. Because of my style of play, and discussions I had with my respected teammates, I chose not to be a victim of the system and see my whole college career go to waste on the sidelines because there was an asterisk next to my name in the program. At the bottom of the team roster it read:

*** = Walk-On**

## The Decision

In December, the last month of my second season, I made up my mind. I was either going to be given a scholarship and play on Saturdays or I was going to transfer. Armed with this decision, and the understanding of how the system worked, I knew I would be transferring in January. The only thing left was the Rose Bowl game January 1, 1990.

Coach April still had me slated as second team on the depth chart on special teams and only an injury to another player would put me in the game. In the month of practice before the game, I was putting together my exit strategy. I had to investigate the NCAA rule regulating a walk-on leaving a program and begin to search for a new school, one that would appreciate me not as a "free player" but one that felt I deserved playing time and a scholarship.

Although the timing was tough, (a week before the game and now in the third week of December), I made my well-considered move. I would approach Head Coach Larry Smith privately and tell him my intentions. On one hand, I was incredibly nervous. On the other, I had mentally departed from the school, which made it a little easier. Just before Christmas Day and following practice, I approached Coach Smith outside the locker room.

"Coach, after spending two seasons on scout team playing with one of the top teams in the nation, I know I can play at this level. With that said I will not be a practice player for four or five years. I am better than that, and I have proven it. Unless you have other plans for me I don't know about, I will be leaving school to go play at another university."

I practiced this speech for hours, usually at night when I was trying to fall asleep. I knew what I had to say, and I had to get it right. I said it over and over again in my mind until my brain shut down and drifted off to sleep. What I did not prepare for was Coach Smith's reaction, which changed the course of my journey—and my life.

**The Promise**

"Tim, I *do* believe in you, and you are one of the best walk-on athletes we have ever had. We do think you will play for us. No, we don't want you to leave. I tell you what; stay here through spring ball. Go through spring ball, and if we feel as a coaching staff that you will be a contributor for us in games, I will put you on full scholarship. If we don't feel you will play much, then I will help you find another school."

Caught off guard and expecting a "good-luck-and-see-you-later" handshake, I was in shock and could only muster the words, "Do you mean it?"

“Absolutely,” the coach said with a smile offering me his hand. We shook on it, and I walked back to the locker room—stunned. I had already made up my mind that I was leaving, and now I was staying—at least for now. I was so confused.

I went home and called Jim Walsh and told him what happened. We talked for hours, and he encouraged me to go see Coach Smith the next day to confirm our conversation and ask how the process would work. If I was going to leave, exactly how was Coach Smith going to help me find another school? Would he be calling other schools in the general area? Division I (D-I) schools? Or was he planning on calling Division II and Division III schools? If so, that would be totally unacceptable. I had already proven I could play at the D-I level. Pawning me off to a D-II or D-III school would not be part of the deal.

Mind you I was only 19 years old, and this whole process scared me to no end. Nervously, I went to the head coach’s office the next day before practice. I expressed my great interest in staying at USC, earning a scholarship, and playing on Saturdays. I had loved becoming a Trojan and wanted to stay one. I did not want to leave, but I originally felt that it was inevitable. Or was it?

Coach Smith reassured me in his office of his commitment to help me find a school that I would want to go to at the D-I level, and he said he would make as many calls as it took to try and help me. When the conversation had ended, I stood up, thanked him, and said he would not be disappointed. I told him I would have an incredible spring practice and no phone calls would be necessary. I ended the conversation with the parting words I had constructed with Jim's help the night before. I remember them vividly: "…and this would be a full scholarship, right?"

Without blinking an eye, Coach Smith answered, "Yes, full scholarship, no partials; I don't believe in them. It is all or nothing!"

With that, I smiled, shook his hand for the second time solidifying our deal and left his office thinking destiny was back under my own control. It was now life in the weight room from January to April. Strength Coach Robb Rogers was on my side. He loved watching me go crazy in practice and knew what was now at stake. I came to him asking to give me the hardest workouts he could for the next three months. He did. After three solid months of training, I felt ready for spring practice and ready to prove my worth to the team and, more importantly, to the coaching staff.

Over a three-week period, spring practice went very well for me. I continued to outperform the expectations of the coaches, and my teammates often made positive comments to me. The final exam would be the Cardinal and Gold game, the last scrimmage of spring practice. With the team divided in half playing in the LA Coliseum in front of 25,000 people, it was show time.

After nearly three hours of battle on that Saturday afternoon, I was fortunate to emerge with stats that made the *Los Angeles Times* the next day. My performance was the best at my fullback position, and I was written up in the newspaper. After the scrimmage, my teammates were making comments in the locker room, such as “Mad Dog in the House!” which was followed by lots of barking. Albeit silly and juvenile, that was my teammates’ way of showing approval. It was an awesome feeling to be respected by my peers, my teammates, my brothers. On that day I truly felt I had graduated from the ranks of “lowly walk-on” to the “scholarship elite.” I was perfectly sure of my rise in status, but I just needed one final confirmation—a last visit to Coach Smith’s office on Monday.

When I awoke Sunday morning, I opened up the *LA Times* newspaper. There was the article on the scrimmage. I got to the meat of the article and it read; “…surprisingly, the leading rusher turned out to be walk-on fullback Tim Lavin, who had eight carries for 64 yards and a touchdown. Ricky Ervins, (who was Rose Bowl MVP back in January, four months earlier), had eight carries for nine yards.”

Filled with confidence on that Monday morning, I went right to Coach Smith’s office. His assistant sat right outside his office door. As I approached her just after 8 a.m., she said with a smile, “Coach said you would be coming by. He’s expecting you.”

She called him on the phone and immediately hung up and told me to go in. I thanked her and walked into his office. Coach Smith rose from his seat and put out his hand. "Congratulations Tim. I am putting you on full scholarship."

With those very words a thousand bricks were lifted off my shoulders, and I beamed with pride and satisfaction as I squeezed his hand for the third time. He told me the paperwork would be done by May, and I could focus on my summer workouts. I thanked him profusely and exited his Heritage Hall office.

After two of the hardest, most physically and mentally challenging years of my life, I left the athletic complex in tears. I was so proud of this accomplishment for a million reasons. I literally had to walk to an isolated area of campus where I wept by myself for several minutes. I had just earned a full scholarship. YES! I would be playing on a regular basis on Saturdays. YES! I was staying a Trojan. YES! What a day! What a spring! What a two-year emotional shuffle!

**Waiting for Paperwork**

In late May, school was ending for summer break so I would periodically poke my nose into the athletic office to find out if my scholarship paperwork had been completed. I was continually told, "...not yet." On the last day of school, Coach Smith told me it would be mailed to my parent's home and to go have a great summer and to work out—hard! I heeded his advice and headed back home to Agoura Hills, an hour drive northwest of L.A.

Several weeks into the summer, no letter had arrived. So I decided to call the office. I was informed that Coach Smith was on summer vacation in Europe and would be back in a couple of weeks. Thanks to my high school coach, Rich Lawson, I scored a summer job at my alma mater, Chaminade College Prep. The job was in the weight room, so I could spend my day working out. This was perfect. I was getting paid to lift weights with high school kids while spending my summer in the weight room. Life was good.

But there was just that issue of not seeing any scholarship paperwork that was still eating at me. I called the office several weeks later and was told the coach was in meetings. I left a message, but no one called back. I called again a few days later, and the coach was at lunch. No call was returned. A few more days went by, and then finally a letter arrived in my mailbox from the athletic department. That letter has a prominent spot in my scrapbook today.

I raced into the house with the biggest smile and a sigh of relief. As the butterflies zipped around my stomach, I opened the letter. It read: "Dear Tim, Congratulations! Because of your efforts we are rewarding you with a half scholarship."

Wait, my eyes just played a trick on me. Let me reread that. "Dear Tim, Congratulations! Because of your efforts we are rewarding you with a *half* scholarship." I started the letter over again not believing my own eyes. "…rewarding you with a half scholarship." I read it again, but the words did not change. A ***HALF*** scholarship? WHAT THE…???

This can't be true; he promised me! DAMN IT!! My joy turned into intense anger in a matter of seconds. I jumped from my chair confused and infuriated. My future was again in doubt, and those two-a-day practices were just around the corner. And now it seemed a little too late in the summer for the coach to start making calls on my behalf to one of those "other" Division I schools.

This was not right; it seemed like a dirty trick. The full scholarship became a half scholarship, and I was not told about it until it was too late in the summer to make a decision to go elsewhere. It was unbelievable! This man looked me in the eye, made a promise, shook my hand three times on that promise, and went back on his word.

To go the entire summer and not to warn me that this was going to happen was inexcusable. Not giving me a chance to transfer to another school was indefensible. To notify me by letter late in the summer of this retreat from his promise was infuriating.

With the letter shaking in my hand, I immediately called Jim Walsh. Jim also was shocked and himself in a state of disbelief. He had coached at this level, in the Pac 10 for Stanford, and he knew this was dishonest, deceitful, and flat out wicked. He talked me into building up the courage to call the coach and confront him. It would be a risk. I was putting my relationship, great spring practice, scholarship, or "half scholarship," and future playing time in jeopardy. My future could be in peril after this call. But my pride and having the truth were at stake too. Without taking the time to sleep on it, I called the coach's office. This time, he took the call.

"Hi Coach Smith. I got the letter, but I am confused. It says half scholarship. And we both know that you promised a full scholarship." I waited for the response. "Yeah, well, you see, the athletic department is having budget cuts and there's nothing I can do about it. How are your summer workouts going?"

I was now 20 years old. The coach was in his early 50s. Yet I knew I was being played, and "the system" was in full swing. I pressed the coach just a tad further while trying not to create tension. "Workouts are going great coach and I can't wait for camp to start. But just real quick—if we can go back to the scholarship question; you stated you did not believe in partials and it was all or nothing." The coach jumped in and put the blame on athletic director Mike McGee.

"Yes, well, with the budget cuts, the athletic director has overruled me, and he is only allowing a half scholarship, and there is nothing I can do about it. So we'll see you at camp in a couple weeks okay, Tim?" Dejected, furious, and not knowing what to say next, I said "OK, sure coach, see you then," and hung up the phone.

I called Jim right away to deliver the news of the conversation I just had with Coach Smith. Jim said to me; "Tim, this is one of the premier universities in the country going to major bowl games every year. There is no way they are having budget cuts! That is a total lie!" I completely agreed it made no sense, but I was stuck. Walsh thought about it for a bit while talking to me and said I should call the athletic director myself, explain the promise that was made by the head coach, and that budget cuts should not be made with the other half of my scholarship I had earned.

Now, fearing a total backlash, I hung up the phone and sat for an hour staring into space. I was at a total loss. I had done everything that was asked of me and more. Yet my own coach was reneging on our deal, and I felt my college career slipping away. The more I endlessly gazed at the floor and ceiling, the angrier I became. I decided, whatever the consequences, I was going to call the athletic director. Taking a deep breath, I dialed the number.

Athletic Director, Dr. Mike McGee, was in a meeting, so I left a message. The next day, a call came from the athletic department. "Tim, this is Marvin Cobb. I am the assistant athletic director at USC. Dr. McGee is busy and he asked me to call you, only I have no idea what this is about. What can I do for you?"

I knew who Mr. Cobb was and believed he really did not know what had happened. So I told my story, the whole story, from beginning to end. Mr. Cobb kept interrupting me asking to clarify parts of the story. He too seemed confused and disheartened.

When finished, I listened intently to Mr. Cobb's response. "Tim, I work in the athletic department, and we are not having budget cuts. Furthermore, even if we were cutting back, we would not do it with a player's scholarship. We don't do half scholarships. You either get a full scholarship or you don't. Also, the head coach makes the decision on who he wants on scholarship, not the athletic director. Dr. McGee does not tell Coach Smith who he can have on scholarship and he definitely would not make a decision to tell the coach to only give a deserving player a half scholarship. That's unheard of."

These brutally honest words were reassuring to me. I could not believe that Mr. Cobb was being so frank and forthcoming. He was not ducking the questions or covering up for anyone. He was sticking up for me and the truth and he didn't even know me.

He then went on and encouraged me to "call the coach out on it." Are you kidding me? Mr. Cobb was telling me to phone the head coach back and *call him out on it*? Are you serious? This couldn't be happening! I was 20 years old and I felt like a ping pong ball bouncing back and forth with advice from all the adults. I'm thinking, "Oh man, if I make this call my career at USC is over, my dreams are dead. I am so screwed."

Mr. Cobb stated; "…I would call Coach Smith, and you tell him you spoke to me, and I told you not to be scared because he's the head coach. Tell him that Mr. Cobb said there are no budget cuts and that he gets the final decision on who gets scholarships and scholarships are full scholarships and we don't do half scholarships." Mr. Cobb went on to tell me how disappointed he was in Coach Smith for reneging on his promise to me. He was really disillusioned and felt awful for me. He encouraged me to stick up for myself.

This was killing me. For sure I will never play here if I make this call. But, I did anyway. I called Coach Smith back.

"Hi Coach; guess who?" I was petrified and used Mr. Cobb's advice verbatim.

I was so nervous I must have sounded like an eight year old kid trying to explain his way out of trouble. My voice was trembling, but I moved forward; "Coach, I spoke to Mr. Cobb who told me to call you back and not to be scared just because you're the head coach."

Smith jumped in, "That's right, no need to be scared, I have an open door policy."

"OK, well, Mr. Cobb said there are no budget cuts going on in the athletic department and that you are the only decision maker on who gets scholarships and there are no half scholarships."

I really wanted to finish with, "Isn't that great news?! I get a full scholarship now! Yeah!" But, I kept my mouth shut as I was shaking, and curled into a ball awaiting Smith's response.

"Tim, Mr. Cobb is obviously unaware of the conversations I have had with Dr. McGee. Being that he is the athletic director, he has the final decision, and he made it. There is nothing I can do about it. That's it."

At that point, I felt I had hit a brick wall. I was defeated and despondently said, "OK, coach, thanks, see you at training camp," as I hung up the phone shaking my head in total disbelief.

**It's not over yet…**

But this story would not end just yet. I went about my business continuing to work out and reported for camp. The first game was days away when a reporter from the *Los Angeles Times* newspaper called me. Apparently someone in the USC media department told the local press the "good news" about one of their walk-ons earning a scholarship. However, they either unknowingly or inadvertently left out the part that it was only a half scholarship. The reporter called my apartment phone and told me he had heard the great news about my earning a scholarship and how impressed he was that a walk-on was able to come to such a prestigious powerhouse football program and earn a scholarship. So the interview began.

Knowing the school's sports information department controlled all interviews and that they had given my apartment phone number to a reporter, I was obviously under the impression that everyone knew I had a half scholarship. During the interview, I recall the reporter being stunned by the "half scholarship" at the Division I level. To boot, he probed me on how this all went down. I told the truth. Big mistake!

The football season just started when the article came out. Within minutes of the early morning hours that weekday, I started receiving phone calls from family and friends who were waking up and surprised to see a giant, full page spread on me in the *Los Angeles Times*. I jumped out of bed and took off for the store two blocks away. I ran there and back. Opening the sports page, my jaw dropped.

A full page article with a giant photo was staring back at me. At first glance, it looked awesome. But then I read it. Turns out the reporter, after hearing my side of the story, called the head coach and asked for a comment in response to reneging on the deal. Coach Smith was quoted as saying, "That is not exactly what happened" referring to the so-called budget cuts that sliced my scholarship in half. Smith also went on to say what a fine player I was and that I had not proven myself in any real game situations yet. He said the half scholarship was a reward for my efforts so far and was intended as a way to provide the incentive to keep me working hard.

I sat there stunned at the coach's comments and could not believe this was for real. A promise was broken, and he hadn't owned up to it. His comment about "not proving" myself "in any real game situation" also rang hollow. His very words to me were: "Go through spring ball, and if we feel as a coaching staff that you will be a contributor for us in games, I will put you on full scholarship."

I had done that. Besides, every year several hundred schools each give scholarships to about 20 to 25 high school students who have yet to prove themselves at the college level. Many get to college but don't pan out. They were great in high school, which scored them a scholarship, but they step on the field at the next level and they fall flat.

In my situation, I had proved I could play with the big boys. I had competed with the stars at USC, some of whom were among the best players in the country. When I got the chance to shine, I had stood toe to toe with them. The coaching staff had conceded that fact, and my fellow teammates acknowledged it too.

Unfortunately, Coach Larry Smith passed away in 2008. But I did reach out to Dr. Mike McGee, USC athletic director during my tenure. When I told Dr. McGee what had happened to me, he said two things: First, he had no recollection of my scholarship situation, which means either that Coach Smith never brought it up with him or perhaps that McGee just forgot what had happened 22 years ago.

However, McGee declared emphatically that never, in his 24 years of being an athletic director, did he ever tell a coach what to do with his allotted scholarships, and it was the coach's responsibility to evaluate talent and award scholarships to players of their choosing. He also said he was very sorry that I went through that experience. I told Dr. McGee that was the first and only apology I had received in 22 years. While McGee had nothing to apologize to me about, I greatly appreciated it anyway and thanked him. In a weird way, it gave me some kind of final validation and closure to the hardest thing I had ever been through as a walk-on.

I did not want to go to practice the day the article came out. When I hit the field that afternoon, only Coach April approached me saying, “Lav, not good, man—not good.” With a pit in my stomach, I assumed, and believed, the whole program was against me. Coach Smith ignored me all day, almost too afraid to get into a discussion that he would win on the basis of his being head coach but, lose on merit, integrity, and basic honesty.

I was sad and angry. At the end of the day, I was incensed that I had been railroaded. But deep inside, I just chalked it up to being a walk-on. It was just another "too good to be true" experience. Perhaps walk-ons were just destined to stay on this miserable path. But that is not what bothered me most.

What humiliated me and crushed my spirit was what I felt it had done to my parents. What was even more devastating than the lies and broken promises to me was what my father now had to do at the eleventh hour. He had to scramble for money. There was another tuition on the table again. And of course, my folks were just devastated for me.

The fall of 1990 was supposed to be the start of my promised full scholarship. My father budgeted accordingly. My folks were not independently wealthy, but my dad did have a good job and got the necessary loans to send his kids to college. My brother Terry was attending Loyola Marymount University in Los Angeles at the same time.

Despite his good salary, it was still a struggle for my father, and coming up with the money would not be easy. My folks had to cut back on everything they did, including traveling to my away games—the first of my games they ever missed.

Originally believing that only Terry's tuition at LMU would be the financial challenge, the now half scholarship letter threw us all for a loop. Not only did I feel like I got punched in the stomach, but my father now had to quickly put together a new budget and figure out how to pay for two college tuitions that fall. He ended up taking out a second mortgage on his and my mother's home in order to pay our tuition expenses.

My father never complained to us about what he must have had to go through as the fees came due. But knowing that he was bending over backwards at the last minute to do everything he could in order to make it all happen for his children broke my heart. It wasn't just the broken promise to me; it was how it had affected my family that hurt the most. I look back on it more than two decades later, and the frustration of that incident still lingers.

I felt isolated and was more miserable with a half scholarship than I was before as a full walk-on. For one thing, I was sure the head coach now would not be making any calls on my behalf. But as a walk-on, I had resigned myself to thinking that I was going to stay for only one last semester, and then transfer to another school in January.

Now, in order to play elsewhere, I would have to go it alone. The coach wasn't going to help. I wanted to be in the best shape of my life, so I practiced as if it were game day throughout the week. I was playing against some of the best players in the country. I went all out every play, every day. I became a wild man at practice and the focal point of one-on-one drills and team scrimmages while still on scout team.

After three weeks of intense practice at the start of the season, an incident occurred that changed everything. In *My Time Has Come* you will read in great detail of the incident that changed the course of my journey. I did something that rallied the entire team behind me and the coaches basically had no choice but to play me. At this stage of the game, it was nearly impossible to keep me from playing on Saturdays, and thanks to Coach Bobby April, I did.

One day, a month into the season, while running special teams, Coach April yelled for me. This time it was to get on the other side of the ball. Within 24 hours of that special day, I received the promotion I was seeking. Not only did Coach April put me on the starting punt-block and punt-return teams, but he also put me on the kickoff, kickoff return, and the hands-teams (on-side kicks).

The next day, I was practicing as the starter on those special teams, but still guarded and skeptical. After practice, I entered the locker room hallway of Heritage Hall and looked up at the travel squad board. My name was on it; it was official. I was traveling and had earned my way onto special teams. I never looked back.

I finished out the season as one of the top special team players of the year. When the season ended, I received a letter from the athletic department that I hadn't expected. When I opened it up, it read: “Dear Tim, Congratulations. Due to your outstanding efforts you are being put on full scholarship.”

***

# Chapter 4
# What's It Like To Be You?

What's it like to be you? A question very few people would ever think to ask a walk-on. How would you know if you never experienced it for yourself or weren't on the other end of a conversation with a walk-on talking candidly about their journey?

So many walk-ons remain quiet about their experiences. Why? The stigma of being a walk-on is somehow looked upon as being shameful. We fear what you are thinking. You see, in our minds, it is almost better to be a regular student than a walk-on. Regular students have nothing to hide; they are just out there having fun in college. They meet new friends, study things they want to study, go to parties, and learn how to perfect bouncing a quarter into a cup.

For the walk-on, the college experience is far different from that of a regular student and also diverges significantly from scholarship athletes. As a walk-on, your stomach is constantly in knots both on and off the field. Everywhere you go, you feel like you are wearing the scarlet letters "WO" on your chest. It's a secret you try to conceal because you don't want to reveal your true identity. The scholarship players walk with pride, in full color. The walk-ons follow in their shadows, in black and white.

You walk scared every day. You meet new people in and out of class, but inevitably someone mentions that you're on the team.

"Oh cool. What position do you play?"

You hope the questions end there. If they do, then you won't be "outed." You want to feel like you are somebody, but you can't; you're too afraid of the dreaded interrogation you know is coming. And then, it happens. The most dreaded question every walk-on fears is hurled from someone's mouth. "Are you on scholarship?"

In that moment, before you can utter a word, a terrifying shame overcomes your entire body. I remember feeling my face turn red in total embarrassment. I suddenly felt like less of a person, the scarlet letters *WO* are now plastered upon my chest for everyone to see, and I just want to leave the room. You go from hoping to feel like a "somebody" to feeling "lower than dirt" in the blink of an eye. Nobody in the room can see your gut is wrenching.

Most people typically don't like to talk about painful times in their life. When you speak to a walk-on they will most likely tell you about the good times they had in their playing days. But, they most likely will leave out the bad times, the painful times, the times they felt ashamed to be on the team only because they had a moniker attached to them. A label not riddled with pride and honor but with fear, shame, and embarrassment.

Internally, you know the coaches think differently about you, many players don't treat you equally, and you walk on eggshells with every step you take and every move you make. How dare you think that you can move up the depth chart? You're just a walk-on! Who do you think you are trying to beat the scholarship guy on this play and show him up! They were recruited! The coaches traveled to their homes and sat in their living rooms telling their parents how incredible their son is in high school, practically salivating over their child, begging him to sign with them.

Externally, you know the student population is thinking, "You are a walk-on because you are not good enough to get a scholarship." Those thoughts and words can make you crumble from within.

And then along comes this walk-on who has the gall, the audacity, the nerve to say, "Hey coach, take a look at me!" But they won't look at you because you're just a walk-on. So you say to yourself, "Ok, watch me!" And the battle is on.

The internal and external battles are a daily grind and truly the only guys who know exactly how you feel are your fellow walk-ons. For me, when I was awarded a scholarship, I got several high fives and verbal adulations from players, coaches, and family. But the most meaningful, powerful reception I got was from fellow walk-on Pat Muldoon. Pat had stopped playing after the previous season and I bumped into him at a party when school first started in September. I had not seen him in about four months, but he had heard about my scholarship. When we saw each other he ran up and threw his arms around me in a giant bear hug. I remember that embrace like it was yesterday because it was so incredibly significant and his words were commanding.

"Lavin, I heard about your scholarship!" he screamed with excitement. "I am so proud of you! You did it! You did it on behalf of the walk-ons!"

Those words resonated deep within me because very few people knew of my struggle, but he did. Other than my family and Jim Walsh, Pat Muldoon's moment with me was extraordinary because of a very special, unbreakable bond of the walk-on brotherhood. In that instant he made me feel like "somebody." I will never forget that moment.

Have you ever met a walk-on? When you are done reading this book you will have a better understanding of the walk-on journey and you will have a new question to ask the next time you see that person. "What's it like to be you?" But, don't expect the answer in a casual chit-chat. If they are going to truly open up to you about what they went through, you'll have to pull up a chair. This will take a while.

***

# Chapter 5

# NCAA: The Hard Cold Facts

To be more than fair, I discovered all the following facts and figures directly from the NCAA.org website and the 2013 – 14 NCAA Division I Manual, effective August 1, 2013. I used no other source other than my humble opinion. What you read below I took straight from the NCAA's own resources.

The NCAA was founded in 1906 to protect young people from the dangerous and exploitive athletics' practices of the time.

Fast forward 107 years to 2013, and more than 450,000 NCAA student-athletes gain skills to succeed on the field, in the classroom and for life. Student-athletes as a group graduate at higher rates than their peers and feel better prepared for life after college.

The NCAA is a member association comprised of 1,066 active member schools; 340 in Division I, 290 in Division II, and 436 in Division III. In general, the purposes of the NCAA are: oversee improvement of intercollegiate athletics, uphold principal institutional control, to formulate and publish rules governing athletics, to legislate, through bylaws or by resolutions, any subject of concern to the members, and to study all phases of competitive athletics and establish standards whereby the colleges and universities can maintain their athletics programs.

Mark A. Emmert, President at the University of Washington, was named the fifth NCAA president April 27, 2010, and took over duties of the office Oct. 5, 2010. He has stressed presidential leadership and values-based action during his tenure. In August 2011, Emmert convened Division I presidents for a leadership summit that focused on stronger enforcement, rules simplification and benefits for student-athletes, among other things.

Founded more than one hundred years ago as a way to protect student-athletes, the NCAA continues to implement that principle with increased emphasis on both athletics and academic excellence.

People need to realize the NCAA office in Indiana does not make the rules. The rules governing NCAA sports are actually developed through a unique membership-led governance system. Using this system, membership introduces and votes on proposed legislation. The national office staff provides administrative help, continuity, research and legal expertise.

However, the NCAA president is a very influential leader who can shape the Association in ways big and small. Sitting university presidents, not athletics directors and coaches, ultimately run the NCAA through its governing system.

The NCAA is a non-profit organization with 96 percent of its expenses benefitting its membership through distributions or services. The remaining funds pay for national office building operations and staff salaries not tied to particular programs.

Much is being written on the current status of the NCAA and the rules that have so many people confused and seeking change. Perhaps we are at a tipping point.

I know from personal experience and research that the 432-page NCAA Division I Manual is extremely confusing. I personally called and spoke to several staff members on numerous occasions seeking help in explaining the rules that concern me. If the rules are difficult to understand and comprehend while reading them and the NCAA staff has a tough time explaining the rules clearly, then how can we expect coaches and young athletes to follow the rules consistently? I guess the question is, has everyone who works at the NCAA and the membership governance read the 432-page manual? And, do they completely understand it?

Today, the NCAA is generating revenue to the tune of over $870 million annually. That number will increase every year due to the TV rights just signed with CBS Sports and Turner Broadcasting, a 14 year deal worth $10.8 billion dollars.

More revenue will continue to pour in via Basketball ticket sales, merchandise, souvenirs, stadium ads, clothing deals, jersey sales, sports marketing, sports films, television shows, DVDs, not to mention the billion dollar video gaming industry and a tiny media deal with ESPN worth $500 Million through 2024.

Bottom line, the NCAA is generating massive amounts of revenue. That revenue is generated by the sacrifices of college athletes, all unpaid.

While the amount of revenue is large, little of the money is retained by the NCAA national office. Again, about 96 percent is distributed directly to the Division I membership or to support championships or programs that benefit student-athletes. The remaining 4 percent goes for central services, such as building operations and salaries not related to particular programs.

The central theme in reading the NCAA Manual is its mission to do what is best for the student athlete, to protect them and help them advance.

Referencing the 2013-14 NCAA Manual, page 3:

**2.2 The Principle of Student-Athlete Well-Being.**

Intercollegiate athletics programs shall be conducted in a manner designed to protect and enhance the physical and educational well-being of student-athletes.

**Refocusing**

While this book is not focused on the financial status of the NCAA, it needs to be put on the table and understood while examining the little-discussed aspect of college football involving the treatment of the game's quintessential student-athlete: The *college walk-on.*

There are a few NCAA bylaws that I call your attention to, which are central to this book. They include the following from the **2013-14 NCAA Division I Manual**:

***16.5.2(C): Training-Table Meals**: An institution may provide only one training-table meal per day to a student-athlete during the academic year on those days when regular institutional dining facilities are open (see Bylaw 15.2.2.1.6). A student-athlete who does not receive institutional athletically related financial aid covering the full cost of board, including a walk-on or partial scholarship recipient, may purchase one training-table meal per day at the same rate that the institution deducts from the board allowance of student-athletes who receive athletically related financial aid covering board costs pursuant to Bylaw 15.2.2.1.6. (Adopted: 1/10/91 effective 8/1/96, Revised: 11/1/01 effective 8/1/02, 5/8/06, 4/26/07).*

Essentially, this rule indicates the meal cost is deducted from the scholarship player's board allowance, and since a walk-on does not get a board allowance, they have to purchase their meals. Scholarship players get their meal for free (like everything else) while the walk-on has to pay for it (like everything else).

The monumental importance of the nutritious training-table meal while performing in the most physically demanding college sport will be discussed throughout this book. Is the code to truly protect ALL student-athletes being followed? Are we only protecting some athletes? Are walk-ons considered student-athletes?

Here is the definition of a student-athlete at the NCAA.

***12.02.9 Student-Athlete****. A student-athlete is a student whose enrollment was solicited by a member of the athletics staff or other representative of athletics interests with a view toward the student's ultimate participation in the intercollegiate athletics program. Any other student becomes a student-athlete only when the student reports for an intercollegiate squad that is under the jurisdiction of the athletics department, as specified in Constitution 3.2.4.5. A student is not deemed a student-athlete solely on the basis of prior high school athletics participation.*

The day a walk-on (recruited or not) steps into the athletic program and reports for duty, he or she becomes, by definition, a student-athlete.

So yes, the walk-on is a student-athlete, but NO, the NCAA will not allow the member institutions to provide invaluable nourishment to help them succeed and protect themselves, unless they open their wallets

***16.4 Medical Expenses.*** *An institution, conference or the NCAA may provide medical and related expenses and services to a student-athlete. (Revised: 1/11/89, 9/6/00, 4/29/04, 8/4/08, 1/19/13 effective 8/1/13).*

May Provide? We know every scholarship player is under the insurance umbrella of the athletic program. But the walk-ons? You guessed it. They are responsible to provide their own insurance. Really? The school can't take care of their own? Shouldn't this rule read, "…must provide medical…?"

***14.5.5 Four-Year College Transfers.***

***14.5.5.1 General Rule.*** *A transfer student from a four-year institution shall not be eligible for intercollegiate competition at a member institution until the student has fulfilled a residence requirement of one full academic year (two full semesters or three full quarters) at the certifying institution. (Revised: 1/10/91 effective 8/1/91,4/14/10).*

If a student-athlete wants to transfer (except in certain situations), the athlete has to sit out one year first. The rule was designed to keep highly-recruited scholarship players from jumping from school to school. The rule also applies to the walk-on who may never see a down of play because his coach doesn't like to play walk-ons. If he transfers he will be handcuffed and punished for a year just because he wanted to keep his dream alive by going to another school.

***3.2.4.4 Academic Performance Program.*** *Each active member is responsible for annually submitting documentation demonstrating its compliance with the academic performance program, including the submission of data for the academic progress rate (APR), the academic performance census (APC) and the graduation success rate (GSR).*

***NCAA.org states how the APR is calculated:***

*Each <u>student-athlete receiving athletically related financial aid</u> earns one retention point for staying in school and one eligibility point for being academically eligible. A team's total points are divided by points possible and then multiplied by one thousand to equal the team's Academic Progress Rate score.*

The APR is based on scholarship players only. The NCAA does not seem interested in the academic achievements of walk-ons. However, the individual schools themselves will certainly include walk-ons in their own internal reports if it helps the overall GPA of the team, which invariably, it always does.

By definition, walk-ons are student-athletes. They are not important enough to eat at training table, but important enough to be penalized if they transfer. Not important enough to cover their insurance, but important enough to include in the member institutions' own GPA and graduation rate system.

Why is there a STOP sign in front of walk-on student-athletes who come from nowhere trying to go somewhere? Why would the NCAA try and limit the chances for a nobody who is trying to become a somebody?

President Emmert is in charge of one of the largest institutions in the world! Like most operations that big, there are rules, policies and procedures that work well and some that don't. There are constant changes going on within the NCAA every year. It has been written that Mr. Emmert and his top officials are working on a major overhaul of the NCAA and how it operates.

I greatly respect the position Mr. Emmert holds and admire him for taking on the challenge. I surely do not envy the task set before him, as everyone is throwing rocks and stones while he is in the middle of trying to reform college sports for the better. I also believe the revenue the NCAA is bringing in is fantastic – IF they truly use it to protect ALL student-athletes.

If I had the opportunity to speak to Mr. Emmert, I would ask him to not let his cabinet members disregard the forgotten walk-on.

There are committees for every group in the NCAA. Yet, there is no voice for the walk-on student athlete. This is not the best we can do, is it?

It has gone on too long with this injustice to the walk-on, the very volunteer-players who shed their blood to make others better. We must end this abomination now. We must stand up and fight as one team. Not a team separated by those who can eat and those who have to fend for themselves. Now is the time to put the past behind us and move forward as one unit … the humiliation must end! The emotional weight must be lifted so that walk-ons can continue their own quest to be the best. In doing so, everybody gets better. When everyone rises up, the bar is set higher. A higher bar means the level of competition gets elevated. How can you lose if everyone is given an equal chance to compete and win?

The rules that adversely affect walk-ons in the NCAA Bylaws Manual create separation, division, and group classification. This naturally erects social barriers. They become a wall that stands between "us and them." A wall separating teammates. The team concept of "we're all in this together" gets thrown away. This wall is not justified. This wall does not unite us. It divides us.

President Emmert, tear down this wall!

***

# Chapter 6

# Welcome, Mr. Walk-On

I remember the first day I reported to training camp. It was early August 1988. The freshmen reported a few days earlier than the upper classmen. We first met in the team meeting room. There were about 30 of us. Roughly 24 were scholarship players, and the rest recruited walk-ons. This was the beginning of a long journey that would shape me and my future, so I was excited and my spirits were high. After the meeting, we were brought down to the locker room and told to find our lockers. It was an L-shaped room with lockers along all the walls, as well as a middle row going down both the vertical and horizontal parts of the L. We walked through the locker room and it was awe-inspiring.

The lockers stood about 7 feet high, 3 feet wide, and 3 feet deep so we could actually sit inside our lockers. This was not like high school. This was big time and I was absorbing it! What a great feeling to look up at these monster lockers and see gold nameplates with the players' last names etched in the cardinal color. I was walking on cloud nine. The horizontal part of the L did not have my name so I kept walking and headed down the vertical row towards the back. When I got to the very tip of the L- shaped room, I found a locker that read, MARINOVICH. And next to his locker, tucked in the corner where the two walls meet, was another locker labeled LAVIN.

Only it was slightly different because my locker was just 5 feet high; there was no beautifully etched nameplate either. My name was written in black magic marker on a piece of white athletic tape. A few inches from my taped name was another last name in black marker on athletic tape. OK, I am sharing a locker. Ordinarily, I would not care. But when I looked around the room, the scholarship freshmen had their own lockers, 7 feet high and with etched nameplates, but the "walk-ons" had to share smaller lockers with their names on easily removable tape. It was just a tad demoralizing, and my spirits took a dip.

On top of each locker sat the shoulder pads. My doubled-up locker had two sets of shoulder pads. My new locker mate was a kicker. We looked at each other as we pulled the shoulder pads off the locker top. In my hands I held shoulder pads the size of when I was in Pop Warner football at age 10. "Well, here are your kicker shoulder pads," I told him. We exchanged shoulder pads and I now held another pair of pads fit for a kicker or maybe a wide-receiver. Interestingly, they were both about the same size and circa 1975. I thought to myself "Well, that is totally strange. I got kicker shoulder pads." Knowing for sure it was a mistake I took my peanut shells over to the equipment room. There, I met Pete, an equipment manager, and introduced myself. Holding the shoulder pads in my hand I told Pete I was a fullback. He said, “Yes, I know.” Perplexed that he was not getting it, I continued: “Ummm, well, I think that maybe, ahhh…can I have bigger pads?” Looking perturbed he flat out told me, “No, get out of here.”

Really? It is my first day and I’m already upsetting the equipment manager and I’m stuck with kicker-size pads? But I just knew I was not going to play fullback at USC with peanut shells from 1975 on my shoulders. A little while later I saw Coach Ray Dorr (who had recruited me as a walk-on) and I expressed my concern by telling him the shoulder pads I got were more suited for a punter, kicker, or maybe a wide receiver. He told me not to go out to the field in those pads and to report to the equipment room right away to get another pair of should pads more suited for a fullback.

Oh man, can you feel the butterflies racing through my stomach? I went back to the equipment room, nervous and trembling; I told Pete that Coach Dorr said to get a bigger set of shoulder pads before I went out to the practice field. Well, Pete was just thrilled to hear that and grabbed the biggest pair of linemen pads he could find and threw them over my head onto my shoulders, slapped down hard on the shells with both hands and said, “There! You happy now?”

Are you kidding me? Really? This is day one of my college career and this is how it’s starting? Apparently Pete was not a fan of being asked by a "walk-on" for—anything. So, I guess asking for a bigger jock strap was out of the question. But I really just wanted some fullback shoulder pads, and I didn't think that was too much to ask. Taking the linemen pads off I handed them back to Pete and timidly said they were too big. He grabbed another pair and threw them on me. They weren't perfect, but close enough, and I said "Brilliant" and bolted out of the equipment room as fast as I could.

Part of me wanted to crawl in a hole and hide. The other part of me wanted to put Pete's head through a wall. I did neither, of course. But in *Dirty Laundry,* later in the book, we will hear more about my next—and last—encounter with Pete.

I realized on day one that this walk-on business was not going to be a fair fight. The scholarship players would get their own 7-foot high lockers complete with etched nameplates, state of the art armor, and would be showered with love and adoration by people at their beck and call. Meanwhile, the annoying walk-ons would have to share smaller lockers, have their name in bright lights on a piece of tape in magic marker, hit the field in subpar equipment, and figure out ways not to get in the way or be a nuisance. Alrighty then—let the games begin!

***

# Chapter 7

# My Fight to Eat

We fight, literally, to prove ourselves. It's an exhausting, grueling battle that we engage in daily. The challenge is unlike anything we have ever gone through, and most people will never experience this rollercoaster in their entire lives. Unless you have "walked-on" in our shoes, you will never truly understand the incredible emotions that run so high, and the physical scars that cut so deep. The following synopsis is indicative of what almost every Division I football player in the country goes through in college.

At the end of practice, many sit in their lockers too tired to move. It takes most players twice as long to get undressed after practice as it does to get dressed before practice. Sitting in your locker, you reach down to untie your shoes with one hand while trying to support yourself with the other. Your fingers and hands are swollen, often bloody, because of tiny cuts in various places. It hurts to grip your shoe so you try and pry it off using your other foot. Peeling off your socks takes longer than you would think. You then have to slice off layers of athletic tape wrapped around your ankles. Try cutting a stack of 50 sheets of paper with a pair of scissors and see how difficult it is. With weakened muscles in your arms and hands it can take several minutes to cut through the tape that has been casted onto your skin for the past 3 hours.

After you manage your way through the post-practice ritual of getting undressed, you stand in the shower and painfully raise your arms above your head as you shampoo your hair. It hurts when you raise your arms. The showers are long just because the water hitting your broken body is the only thing that brings you some relief.

You put your street clothes on and leave the athletic building. Another 5-hour football experience is in the history books, and you're starving. You watch the scholarship players walk to the training table cafeteria. Reluctantly, you part ways with your brothers because you are not allowed to eat with them.

The first time I remember being told I was not allowed to eat with my teammates I didn't believe it. One of the GAs (graduate assistant coaches) entered the dining hall after practice on the first official day of school and asked the walk-ons to leave because of a rule that stipulated walk-ons were not allowed to eat at training table once school started.

I thought it was a dumb joke. Freshmen got jokes played on them from time-to-time, and I just thought the GA was in on this one. This couldn't possibly be a real rule. In fact, I was so sure it wasn't true, I ignored the coach with a half-hearted laugh and continued eating—for about 10 seconds.

I had never heard of this rule, it was never brought to our attention, and the GA was sent in to do the dirty work after almost four weeks of eating together as a team. He had to tell us that, as walk-ons, we were no longer allowed to be part of the team at the training table. We had to find another place to eat. Somewhere, anywhere, just not in the coaches' and scholarship players' only VIP dining hall.

The GA was relentless. With a straight-face and stern voice he explained the rule to me. Since I truly did think this was a cruel joke, I did not leave the dining hall immediately like the other walk-ons. I stayed and asked the coach over and over again; “Are you serious? Are you serious?” It was not a heated discussion, but we were not whispering either. He was not budging, and I was not believing.

Although I kept myself under control, I was beyond furious that a GA was sent to tell me I was no longer welcome at training table to nourish my body with my teammates as I had been doing for the past four weeks. I remember saying something to the effect of, “Wait a minute. I've spent 16 hours a day, seven days a week with my teammates for over a month. I have gone to every meeting, watched dozens of hours of film, got dressed in the same locker room, put on the same uniform, got taped in the same training room, went out to practice and gave everything I had just like the other players. I left my emotions, my blood, my bruised body, and gallons of sweat on that field. And you are now telling me that for the rest of the season, I can't eat at training table with my teammates?"

Having stood up during this conversation, we were now starting to make a scene. I looked around the room to get confirmation that this was a joke. But no one was laughing. Almost 85 scholarship players were all sitting, eating, and watching this go down. The room was quiet except for the GA trying to convince me I was no longer allowed in the very room where I had spent so much time with my teammates.

When the GA finally convinced me this was not a joke, I left my plate of food on the table and walked through the private dining hall. The whole team watched me exit. This was the longest and most humiliating walk I had ever taken in my life. I felt everyone's eyes on my back as I walked out of the room. I went from feeling like a teammate to a leper in a matter of minutes. My body was filled with anger and tears.

The training table rule went into effect when the school year started. During August, the team and everyone associated with the football program ate together in a private dining hall. However, once the campus cafeterias officially opened to feed the student body at the start of the school year, the walk-ons had to leave their teammates and go elsewhere.

I quickly learned that the *student managers* and *student trainers* were allowed to eat at training table. They worked hard, no question. The managers had to meet with the coaches before we hit the field to get the practice script. They had to put all the balls, cones, blocking bags, and sleds together on the field. They had to understand the order of practice for the day and know what hash mark to place the football on before each play or drill. They were running all over the field with two, three, or four footballs cradled in their arms with whistles going off left and right. I respected the managers. They were out there with us. As fellow students, we went to classes with them. They were part of the team too. They did not get paid, but as a thank you perk for their dedication they were allowed to have a free training-table meal after practice.

The student trainers were learning how to tape ankles and give treatment to players who were injured. They brought medical supplies, ice, and water to the field for practice. They put in long hours too and were part of the team. Nor did they get paid. But as a thank you perk for their dedication, they also were allowed to have a free training-table meal after practice.

This was supposed to be one big family. It seemed that way until the day school started in September. Then the team broke apart, and the walk-ons—and only the walk-ons—now had to fend for themselves.

Many walk-ons accepted the rule and went to other dining establishments after practice. Me? I wasn't buying it. I went to training table anyway. It's supposed to be policed by the coaches. The food service staff certainly does not know who is who. So the coaches go there to eat and look around for any walk-ons to kick out. For many weeks, I dodged the coaches, hid behind walls and under tables. My scholarship brothers covered for me because that's what teammates do.

However, the inevitable happened. One day a coach spotted me. "Hey Lavin, you're not supposed to be in here." Thanks, coach. I turned and walked away feeling alienated and dejected—again. My feeling of being a part of the team was slipping away. I was both sad and mad, and my stomach was a mess.

At training table, you were allowed to fill a doggie bag to bring home so you could munch on some healthy snacks later in the evening. Well, our scholarship brothers would make several to-go boxes and bring them downstairs to the waiting walk-ons hiding behind walls so the coaches would not see. That is how we got our dinner. Our brothers took care of us.

How sad it is to be a starving walk-on after a long practice. You shower up and walk gingerly to the training table cafeteria area. Your body is sore from the punishment, but that's football. You're dying to jump into a hearty meal. Instead, you're forced to hide behind a wall so a coach won't see you crouching nearby and get suspicious. You anxiously sit 30 to 40 minutes like you're waiting in a soup kitchen line. The to-go boxes arrive, one-by-one. The scholarship guys have finished their meals and hand off doggie bags to the walk-ons.

The walk-ons had to select different players to ask each day, so the same guys were not always bringing out tons of food. If there were 10 walk-ons hanging out behind the wall together, you could be sure that at least 10 scholarship guys would be leaving the dining hall with bags of food to discretely hand off to their starving walk-on brothers.

As I interviewed scores of players from across the country, both scholarship and walk-on players alike; they all had the *same* stories. The doggie bag handoff play apparently is repeated nationally at every school. That is a huge message. It says so much about team unity. No matter if a rule tries to break us apart, we are teammates, and we are trained to look after each other. If you put up an unjust wall, humans find a way to tear it down. It's a universal truth.

I was on scholarship my last two years, and you better believe I looked after the walk-ons. Even while on scholarship, I still felt part of the walk-on fraternity. It gave me great satisfaction to make a hot meal and hand it off to a patiently waiting walk-on around the corner of the dining hall after practice. What a shame we had to do that.

I spoke to one coach at a university in the Midwest. He told me he did the same thing as a player in the 1980's and he saw it as a coach as well, years later. He knew what was going on but pretended to be looking the other way if he happened to walk up on guys holding boxes of food. Another coach, also on staff with a Division I school on the West Coast right now, told me he felt so bad for walk-ons that *he* would make several to-go boxes and hand them off to waiting walk-ons. He remembers specifically how the team used to practice at their game field facility (far away from the school site) on Fridays before games. They brought in training table to the stadium for the players to eat after practice. He remembers the outside temperatures being 104 degrees, but the walk-ons were not allowed in the dining area of the stadium. They waited outside in the heat. Sick to his stomach, he rallied several scholarship players and they all made to-go lunches and took them outside to the hungry walk-ons.

Another former player I spoke with thought the training table rule was so unjust that he would ask the catering staff for big green trash bags and he would make 10 to 20 meals. Like Santa Claus, he would meet the walk-ons outside, hiding behind walls, and hand out their presents. One would think they were well-deserved and warranted, but not the NCAA Rules Cabinet.

These coaches and several former players asked me not to use their names for fear of retaliation from the NCAA for this rule violation since they are still coaching at the Division I level today. After I interviewed scores of players and coaches from dozens upon dozens of Division I-A and I-AA schools, I found this to be a widespread and established practice. In fact, I could not find anyone at any institution who knew this rule was strictly followed.

I would like to say to every scholarship player who has ever looked after his fellow walk-on teammate with no food, "Thank you for taking care of him! Thank you for doing the right thing." That is what teamwork is all about. It may be bending or breaking the rules, but I doubt there is a coach, player, or fan across the United States of America that thinks this NCAA policy is a good rule.

***

# Chapter 8
# Necessary Nutrition

Why do walk-ons, or any players for that matter, need to eat properly while training at the highest level of their sport? After much research and many interviews with individuals, I narrowed down my discussion and exploration with Michael Smith, owner of CrossFitHB in Huntington Beach, Calif.

Smith is coaching major college and professional athletes today. More than just physical training, Coach Mike spends great time and detail with his athletes on the nutritional significance of their training. Many of his students drivc long distances to specifically work and learn from him.

There are hundreds of nutritional books on the market today. I asked Coach Mike to break it down for me, short and sweet, for the purpose of this limited space.

Put quite simply, there is no way to out train poor nutrition. As Coach Mike explained to me, and what thousands of other health professionals attest to, you cannot expect exercise to be the only catalyst to a healthy body. You cannot outwit your body with rigorous exercise and poor nutrition. As Coach Mike tells it, "you cannot exercise your way out of a bad diet."

There are thousands of websites and books written about proper nutrition and health so all I will do here is list some critical key points to confirm my stance about walk-ons eating at training table. With Coach Mike's help, I was able to understand, and hopefully can explain, the process better.

Your body must be in balance between the anabolic and catabolic state. Catabolic is when you tear down your body through rigorous activity, and anabolic is building yourself up stronger through proper nutrition and rest. When training, (especially at the highest competitive levels of sports), your body goes into a catabolic state as you push yourself to the limits through demanding exercise.

In order for your body to recover and grow stronger, your body *must* slip into an anabolic state. You can only do this through proper rest and nutrition. If you cheat your body out of either one of those equally vital processes, you will not grow stronger and will level off becoming more susceptible to injury. You actually start fighting against your body rather than helping it advance. Instead of taking two steps forward during exercise and recovery, you take one step back.

Recovery is just as important as working out. There is no such thing as overtraining, only "under-recovery." That means that you cannot compromise recovery by working out harder. You can slave away in the gym and practice field, but without the proper recovery methods of rest and nutrition, you will be moving sideways and backwards consistently.

Training table exists for a reason. Olympic athletes must focus on their training table as much as they do proper rest and working out. College scholarship athletes are expected to perform at the highest level of competition, and training table is provided to them to help accomplish this. But, it's not offered to walk-ons.

As previously stated, walk-ons are forced to pay for everything. When on a shoestring budget, fast processed foods and sugary drinks are the cheap alternative to the more expensive, unprocessed foods at training table. Poor food choices lead to broken recovery, low energy and fatigue. Your body is rigidly timed and must absorb the nutrition it needs to slip into the recovery, or anabolic state. If too much time is spent in the catabolic state, the low energy and fatigue will lead to a much higher risk of injury.

Yet, walk-ons are vital to the team and critical to helping the scholarship athletes perform better. They are asked to go toe-to-toe and leave everything on the field. With nothing in their bellies but fire, grit, and determination, they give everything they can and lay it all out on the line. But, when it comes time for recovery, they are left in the dust like malnourished cattle and forced to pay for the nutrition their bodies desperately crave while scholarship players, coaches, student trainers and student mangers all are given highly nutritious meals for free.

This is the biggest injustice in the entire NCAA rule book, and it must be overturned. This is not about fair or unfair. This is about health and safety. This is about giving all athletes the necessary and proper ammunition to perform at their expected level. Proper nutrition is as important to athletes as getting your ankles taped, studying playbooks, lifting weights, watching films, and icing down a bruised and battered body. It is all part of the big puzzle. Walk-ons have a piece missing from the puzzle and it's the biggest mistake happening in college football today.

The NCAA has a duty to protect these athletes. Proper nutrition is vital to peak performance. To deny walk-ons the necessary nutrition to do their jobs is setting them up for injury and failure.

***

# Chapter 9
# Dirty Laundry

Every day after practice, you would turn in your mesh laundry bag, a fishnet type sack made with dime-sized holes. Your bag contained your undershirt, shorts, socks, jock, tights—whatever you had worn beneath your equipment during practice. A label had your last name and jersey number in black magic marker. Massive washing machines washed scores of bags after practice.

The equipment room was off-limits to the players, and we had to report to a small window in the hallway to get our clean bags the next day. The window adorned metal bars creating a cage-like look.

Every day you would walk up to the cage and ask for your laundry bag by saying your jersey number. I was taught by my parents to *always* ask for something by saying "please" and to *always* say "thank you." It was second nature to me.

When I asked for my laundry bag before practice, I would say, "37 please." When it was pulled off the shelf from behind the cage and thrown to me, I would respond with "thank you," and be on my way. All too often, other players would walk up and bark out commands demanding to get their bags. "Yo, Pete, get my bag!" Without hesitation, Pete quickly moved to the shelf, grabbed their bag and tossed it on the counter sliding it under the caged bars to the waiting scholarship player.

Pete knew the sound of their voices too. He would not even have to turn around to see who was yelling at him. He didn't need to hear them say their number. If he heard, "Pete, get my bag! I'm late for my meeting! Hurry up!" he would race to grab the bag and bring it to the window in two seconds flat. These of course were scholarship players barking for their bags. Obviously, not all scholarship players were rude and obnoxious. In fact, most were not. It was only a small group who created that bad impression.

Many times, I would ask for my bag and patiently wait…and wait…and wait. Then I would hear a voice behind me: "Get my bag, Pete!" Sure enough his bag came first, then the other guy behind him would yell, and then yet another. After those three or four guys got their bags, I would finally receive mine. The anger grew inside me.

If a walk-on was the only person standing at the window, he would usually have to wait for the equipment manager to finish adjusting a strap on a pair of shoulder pads or putting in a new screw in a helmet. But, if a scholarship player walked up to the window behind the walk-on, the manager dropped what he was doing and his bag hit the counter. After weeks and then months of seeing this happen continuously, my blood was beginning to boil.

With each passing day, my anger grew, but I remained silent. Finally one day, I could no longer hold it inside, and I completely exploded. I walked up to the cage and asked for my bag. “Thirty-seven please.” Five seconds passed, then ten. “Yo, Pete, get my bag” shouted a voice from over my shoulder. In less than three seconds, the bag belonging to the voice behind me was at the window. I lost it! I completely lost all of my self-control and short of turning green, I became the Incredible Hulk!!!

I reached under the window cage and tried to grab Pete by the shirt. At the top of my lungs I screamed: “You mother f…, how dare you! How dare you treat walk-ons like we don't exist!”

I was trying to crawl through the 8-inch gap between the counter and the bottom of the metal bars while I continued screaming. “You treat us like second-class citizens, and you bend over for the scholarship guys!”

I was swinging my arms and reaching in vain to grab Pete as he backed away from the window and looked at me in terror while this psycho walk-on tried to come after him. I managed to get my head and arms under the bars but, as I tried to slide through the gap and get into the equipment room I could not go any further than my chest. I continued swinging at him while reaching, trying to grab any article of his clothing.

Within seconds, my teammates heard the commotion and came running down the hall to see what was happening. My rage continued as I screamed, "Every day I say 'please' and 'thank you,' yet you still treat me like sh&%!! You bend over for the scholarship guys. Okay, I get it now—you like to be disrespected and treated like a jock washer! Okay, fine, I won't treat you with respect anymore!"

I kept pulling myself in, trying to squeeze my body through the gap under the cage and reach him. He was far enough back that I couldn't hit him with my fist, but he watched in horror as I unleashed a tirade of expletives. I am not sure what would have happened had I grabbed him, but I do know it would not have been pretty. I am sure I would have been dismissed from the team, and probably the University.

Since my body was partially under the bars, and I was screaming at the top of my lungs, several of my teammates came running over to the window to subdue me. Across the hall, the players in the training room who were having their ankles taped all jumped off their tables and raced into the hallway to see what was happening. Before I knew it, I had four or five guys grabbing my lower body trying to pull me out from between the counter and the metal bars. Pulling both of my legs and bear hugging my waist, they were yelling, "Whoa! Whoa! Whoa! Calm down Lavin! Calm down!"

I tried to push my teammates off me with one hand while holding the end of the equipment room counter with the other.

There was a huge struggle as I refused to let go. My strength was coming from pure adrenaline. I heard, "Stop, stop! Let it go, Lavin, let it go! Lav, Lav stop it! Let it go…."

They finally pried my fingers from the counter and the bars and dragged me down the hallway. About 10 to 15 other players surrounded us and stood there in silence and shock. My whole body was shaking. Holding me by my arms, several players escorted me to my locker. I tried to get dressed for practice, but there was too much adrenaline racing through my body. It was an unrecognizable feeling, and it took several minutes sitting in my locker to simmer down enough to get my shoulder pads on and tie my shoelaces with my trembling fingers.

I could hear the players talking about what just happened, but I couldn't make out what they were saying. I was in such a focused state; I could hear voices without hearing words. At that moment, I was a different person, incapable of comprehending the sounds around me. I knew they were talking about me, but I couldn't respond. I was in a zone I don't ever remember being in before. I was thinking of the way I felt and how incredibly angry I was. It was months of pent-up anger unleashed all at once. My feelings were mixed with aggression and fear. I was furious with how walk-ons were treated, but I was also scared when I realized that going after an equipment manager could be grounds for dismissal from the team. The emotions in me were so intense I was in a fog.

Once dressed, I walked out onto the practice field ready for battle. When I got to the front gate and stepped on the grass, I took off running on our daily trot around the field. Only my trot was more like a sprint. I could not wait until our full scrimmage so I could unleash my anger in full speed competition. I believe I got into six or seven fights that day on the field. It was my way of blowing off steam.

When practice had ended, I turned my motor off and hit the showers. My stomach was in knots. I was still afraid I was going to be called into the coach's office to discuss my outburst before practice. It never happened. The coaches were never told, or if they were, they never confronted me.

Ironically, what did happen was a total transformation of attitude in the equipment guys and players alike. From that day on, whenever I would walk to the cage before practice, my bag was almost at the window before I could open my mouth. "37 ple…" and my bag hit the counter. "Oh wow, thank you!" I also heard other guys saying "please" and "thank you" as I approached the cage. I was shocked. I think the equipment guys were too. They suddenly were being treated differently, with more respect, and just the whole vibe felt more positive and upbeat—like we are all in this together.

For the next 3½ years, there was never another problem and most everyone was using the "polite system" when asking for their bags before practice. That was an awesome learning experience for all of us. Oh, and today, when I see Pete, we act like old friends as if nothing had ever happened.

***

# Chapter 10

# No Gifts for You

When the 1988 regular season ended, we were headed to the Rose Bowl. The showdown would take place January 1, 1989, against Michigan.

It was now December, and bowl-game preparations had begun. For the last four and a half months we had practiced. Nothing was unusual at the time. There were mandatory weight room workouts, hours of meetings, and watching films. The whole team was part of this journey. The scholarship players and the walk-ons were all in the same boat doing the same things. This was a total team effort. We were in it to the end, or so the walk-ons thought.

When Christmas break came in mid-December, the student body went home for the 3-week vacation. What a great time to be a college student! Three weeks of relaxing, hanging out with family and high school friends, and partying like it was 1999. All except for those associated with the team. The football players, managers, coaches, and trainers stayed behind on campus. There was no break for any of us. It was all football, 24/7. The team was given Christmas Day off and those who lived close enough would drive home for 24 hours. They brought teammates home with them who lived far distances away so they did not have to be stuck in a dorm room alone on December 25th. It's a t*eam thing*. You never leave your teammates behind. Within 24 hours, the entire team was back on campus, back on the field, and it was back to business.

Strangely enough, the walk-ons were pulled aside after one practice and told that NCAA rules allowed only 95 players to travel and suit up for the bowl game on January 1. What? Everyone knew that the rule for the travel squad team during the season was 60 players. But for a bowl game, we were certain that everyone got to go.

The walk-ons received a letter from the head coach. It read, "…NCAA rules only allow us to travel 95 players to the Bowl game." It went on to say that with 85 scholarship players, they could bring 10 walk-ons to the game, and that would be decided "by seniority." The junior and senior walk-ons were allowed to go. But the rest of the 15 or so freshman and sophomore walk-ons would be left behind. I can't tell you how delighted I was to have had no-Christmas vacation, help the team prepare for the Rose Bowl for three weeks and then be told to go home or sit in the stands. It was unbelievable.

Two decades later, as I researched what the rule was for the 1988-89 season with an NCAA official (Jennifer Royer, Associate Director of Public and Media Relations), I found that no such rule existed. In fact, every player, including all walk-ons, should have been able to travel to that game, stay in the team hotel the night before, and suit up on game day.

After practice on December 30th, the walk-ons were thanked for their effort and told they could go home. They did give us the option, however, of going to the game as a spectator. If you wanted to go to the Rose Bowl game, there would be one ticket for you at the Will Call ticket booth, but only one.

I lived within driving distance of the Rose Bowl, and for whatever reason, I was a stupid freshman, I decided to go. After an hour or more drive, I got my ticket at Will Call and sat in the end zone near the top of the stadium—by myself. No other walk-ons sat near me. Either they chose not to go, or their seats were elsewhere. Regardless, I sat by myself not knowing a soul around me and watched my teammates on the field and on the sidelines. I was part of that team, but I sure didn't feel like it.

Michigan won the game, and a week or so later we were back on campus for a team meeting. Even with the loss, all the players still got Rose Bowl rings, watches, and lots of swag. We all got fitted for a Rosc Bowl ring, even the walk-ons. Well, at least we will get the same reward the team gets for going to this prestigious bowl game, right?

When the gifts were given out to the scholarship players, coaches, managers, trainers, team doctors, and all athletic department personnel, they all received the Rose Bowl ring—a gorgeous 75th Anniversary Rose Bowl watch, a beautifully embroidered jacket, a travel duffel bag, and a great looking sweat suit outfit. The walk-on players received the ring, a t-shirt, and a hat.

As it was explained to the walk-ons by the head coach, there was not enough money to buy the watches and other apparel items for the walk-ons.

***

# Chapter 11

## The Coaching Mindset

To be perfectly clear, not all coaches are cut from the same cloth. Many have had an incredible impact on my life, and I love them dearly for that, but there are far too many coaches who fall prey to the coaching mindset that “my way is the right way” (also expressed as “my way is the *only* way.”)

With regard to coaching the basics, many coaches learn a particular way early on and rarely deviate from this mindset. It’s who they are, who they have become. It is still shocking to me how many college coaches overlook walk-ons or how many NFL coaches seem to overlook players with off-the-field “issues.”

It is alarming to me how some coaches break their own rules. The bottom line is this: you play your best player! Who *is* the best player? If the walk-on is the best player at his position, he *still* may not play because the coach is struggling with a personal problem. He recruited Player A and gave him a scholarship. While Player B walked-on and beat out Player A. That doesn't sit well with the coach.

Coaches are a funny breed. They are hell-bent on being right. And when they are wrong, they will go out of their way to keep trying to be right because to accept being wrong means that some kid came out of nowhere and outplayed the guy they recruited, which is a personal affront to their decision-making capabilities.

And so the walk-ons suffer. Too many coaches are caught up in what is *supposed* to happen that they overlook the obvious when it is staring them in the face. The kid they spent years recruiting and thousands of dollars on is *supposed* to be a Blue-Chip star. He is supposed to come on the college field and make a statement. He is supposed to out-play all the others and start. He is supposed to be one of the best players of all time at his position. He is supposed to make the coach look like a genius for recruiting him.

Keep in mind this is a yearly practice. Every year the staff recruits new players thinking that the next player is even better than the previous year's big-time recruit. No matter what the position, there are new players every year who are *supposed* to be the "next best thing" known to football. Every year, there are *supposed* to be Blue-Chip All-Stars coming in to shine.

Take a position, any position—let's say quarterback. If a player is going to walk-on at quarterback, he not only needs to outperform the four or five Blue Chip All-Star scholarship quarterbacks ranging from freshmen to fifth-year seniors, but he also has to hurdle the coaches mindset that a no-name "walk-on" has come out of nowhere and is playing better than the "stars" he has recruited over the last five years! That is an enormous hurdle.

The hard cold reality is that coaches recruit the best they can find every year. And one day, along comes a walk-on who defies the odds, steps up and shows he has every right to be on that field because his performance outshines those with the long list of high school accolades. He is *not* supposed to be this good; otherwise he would have received a scholarship somewhere. For whatever reason, he didn't. But he is here now.

It is at this moment that I wish all coaches would consider accepting reality instead of fighting or pushing back against the situation. I wish more of them would just embrace it. Let the competition flow, and let the best man win!

Unfortunately, stubborn coaches see this competition and are secretly, internally saying, "Where the hell did this walk-on kid come from? I can't play him in front of *my* scholarship guy!"

To the college bound, my advice is this. When you discover that walking-on is the path you will take, do your homework. Use the Internet as your best friend. Research the colleges and universities and specific coaches who have a history of rewarding walk-ons with playing time and scholarships. Find out which coaches don't give very many scholarships to walk-ons and which ones take them away to make room for someone else. Trust me, it happens.

Also, go to my website, www.Walk-OnU.com. I post the stories about the coaches who admire and respect walk-ons, coaches who give them opportunities to play on Saturday, and reward them with scholarships that they earned.

At this time the NCAA rule is that scholarships are renewable every year. This puts even more control in the coaches' hands. The website will report on the coaches who do not renew a walk-on's scholarship and find out why. If a walk-on does not have an "earned" scholarship renewed because of "issues" either on or off the field, then his scholarship, in my opinion, should be pulled. As a coach, I would pull it myself if a kid suddenly went from the hardest working player to someone with an attitude unbecoming that of a model player. Cop a poor attitude, get bad grades, display improper behavior on or off the field, and your scholarship is gone! I support that 100 percent. I'm the biggest proponent of walk-ons, but I would be the first to pull a scholarship from a guy who went south.

But if a coach pulls a scholarship from a deserving walk-on to make room for another player, then we will be reporting on that loud and clear at Walk-OnU.com in hopes that the exposure will discourage the coach from ever pulling that stunt again.

***

# Chapter 12
# JUNIOR SEAU

My first two years at USC (my true freshman and redshirt freshman years) were spent on scout team offense. I was practicing against a Trojan defense that was ranked at the top of college football. We had future NFL players litter that defense: Mark Carrier, Chris Hale, Dan Owens, Pat Harlow, Matt Willig, Ernie Spears, Tim Ryan, Scott Ross, Kurt Barber, and another guy by the name of Junior Seau.

I was a tailback in high school. When I walked-on at USC, running back coach Clearance Shelmon made me a fullback on day one. I had expected that. However, my frame was still that of a tailback. I might have weighed 195 lbs., with 5-pound weights in my thigh-pad pockets. The other fullbacks on the roster were all 225 lbs. or more. I looked like a tailback and had to play scout team fullback and play against a top rated defense of all-stars. Welcome to major-college football.

Also on day one, I realized I needed to hit the weight room hard if I were ever going to compete. Working out and eating like never before, I slowly put on more weight and muscle. What was already big was my desire to prove that I was no walk-on-scout-teamer-for-life player. I knew I would spend at least one, and probably two years on scout team, but I also wanted the coaching staff to take notice that I could play and that I intended to move up the depth chart ladder.

Tuesday, Wednesday, and a few Thursdays were our full-pads, hard hitting scrimmage days. Those were my game days—my time to shine—and it was the only opportunity I would have to show I could play. While running the opponents' plays, I scrimmaged against our first and second team defenses. That was challenging, but it gave me a huge advantage. I got better—fast.

Junior Seau was my favorite target. I knew Seau was considered one of the best linebackers in the country, and he certainly was the best player on our defense. Knowing that, I wanted to go against him as often as possible. Every chance I had to block Seau, I would get low and give him the most powerful block I could. As a result, Junior Seau and I got into more fist fights with each other than we probably did with anyone before or since, with the exception of maybe our respective brothers while growing up, (but that doesn't count).

Honestly, Junior and I got into scuffles or full-on fights almost daily. On average we fought at least three to five times a week. Over the course of two seasons, plus preseason and spring football, I estimate Seau and I fought with each other well over 100 times. That's a lot of fighting. Unlike a few other players I fought with who carried the grudge into the locker room, Junior never did. In fact, he and I had total respect for one another and always gave each other a pat on the helmet when our fights were broken up or a high-five back in the locker room. We never talked trash to each other. Our fights were because of the heat of the battle, one guy getting the best of another guy and frustration taking its course. Our fighting in practice usually only lasted a few seconds, 10 seconds max, before players or coaches would step in and break it up. In full gear, it is tough to really hurt someone and we never did injure each other.

However, after some of our most brutal and long-lasting fights, Seau would always come up to me in the locker room and give me a hug. Bruised and battered with nothing left in my tank, Seau would always say to me, "Way to go buddy, way to go." Seau called everyone "buddy." Even after our biggest fight during the two years we were going at it, Junior was so gracious after practice with me. At one point, Junior broke a small bone in his wrist and wore a cast for a couple of weeks. That didn't stop him from playing. The trainers just wrapped his cast with lots of padding, and Junior was back on the field wielding his cast around like a club. I was the recipient of that club.

During one of those cast-club days, Seau and I got into one of our most violent fights ever. I remember it was the biggest, knockdown, drag-out fight we ever had. I got the better of Seau on the play and pushed him back over the pile. He was so angry that he slugged me in the helmet with his cast club fist. I punched him back and the fight was on. We stood toe-to-toe throwing punches at each other, and then, with all the grabbing of the facemasks, we both fell to the turf, rolling around, punches flying, his cast club pounding my helmet. Thankfully, my helmet stayed on. It took several players and coaches to break us apart because neither one of us would let go. Finally, we were pried apart and sent back to our respective huddles.

After practice, I went to the locker room and sat down completely exhausted. I was too tired to get undressed. Seconds later, I saw Junior Seau approach my locker. I immediately thought the fight was going to resume in the locker room, and for a second, I considered putting my helmet back on. I stood up as Seau approached me, and yes, I was nervous. But Junior opened his arms and bear hugged me. Speaking into my ear Seau said this: "You sure don't play like a walk-on. Don't ever give up Lav, don't ever give up. I love your passion."

I will never forget those words.

Seau then sat down next to me, and we talked. He told me straight up that he respected me and that I deserved to be at the other end of the field (with the first and second team offense, not on scout team). He also said I hit harder than the guys that were in front of me on the depth chart. Coming from him that was one of the best compliments I ever received at USC. He told me to "never give up and keep doing what you're doing." I did. Seau was the fifth pick in the first round of the NFL draft in April 1990, and I received my football scholarship effective in September.

Because I had so much to prove, Junior Seau was the best person to prove it against. When I got a good block on Junior and kept him from making the tackle, it was extremely rewarding and gratifying. When Junior shed my block and made the tackle, I knew what I did wrong and learned quickly how to better position myself to get the leverage I needed to be successful on the next play. Let's just say I went through one hell of a learning curve, but I got better every day because of Seau. In fact, he was my greatest teacher. There is nothing like experience. You can talk all day long in the meeting rooms drawing X's and O's on the chalk board, you can watch thousands of hours of film. But no off-the-field training prepares you better than on-the-field experience. My "on-the-job-training" was going up against one of the greatest linebackers in football history. For that, and the fact we were teammates, I will remain forever grateful. I am privileged to have been in more physical confrontations with Seau than probably anyone else during his career—college or pro. I am honored that I got to practice against him and I got better because of playing with one of the greatest linebackers the sport will ever know.

I reached out to Junior to interview him for this book and talk about our exchanges on the football field at USC. He said he would do it, but it never happened. Unfortunately, in May 2012, Junior Seau committed suicide at his home in Oceanside, California.

***

# Chapter 13
# Irreparable Harm

In early January 2013, it was reported by the researchers at the National Institute of Health (NIH) that Junior Seau's abnormalities in his brain were consistent with chronic traumatic encephalopathy (CTE).

NIH, based in Bethesda, Maryland, said the findings from tests on Seau's brain were similar to those from autopsies of other people exposed to repeated head injuries. CTE is described by researchers at Boston University as a disease that is commonly associated with repeated blows to the head. It has been linked to multiple systems including memory loss, dementia, and depression. The condition often develops into serious symptoms that mimic Parkinson's disease, ALS, or even Alzheimer's.

In the span of just two years, 2011–2013, at least six NFL players committed suicide: Junior Seau, Dave Duerson, Ray Easterling, Kurt Crain, OJ Murdock, and Jovan Belcher. Autopsies of Seau, Duerson, and Easterling found that all three showed signs of CTE caused by repeated blows to the head.

The subject of head trauma in sports is a major hot topic. The amount of recent information in the media from researchers and medical professionals would fill an encyclopedia. We can only touch on the topic here in order to bring up an important point.

Much of the media on the subject of CTE seems to revolve around professional football players. It is critical to recognize that concussions happen more frequently at the college level. Yes, there are a lot more teams and players for sure. However, the NFL players also have the Collective Bargaining Agreement (CBA) on their side.

The CBA states that NFL teams can only have 14 full padded practices per year. Eleven of those practices must occur during the first eleven weeks of the regular season and the final three can happen over the next six weeks. There is no CBA for NCAA Student Athletes. Some college football teams have 14 full padded practices by week five or six and will have more than 20 or even 30 live practices if they go to a bowl game. That's a lot of hitting that college athletes endure. The CBA may not be the only reason there is less hitting in the NFL. While many coaches love live action scrimmaging in college, most coaches at the NFL level seem to believe the less hitting the better.

Today, most NFL coaches teach going hard off the snap of the ball for the first two or three steps, but they have to stay balanced and not fall to the ground. "That is how we judge athletes. We look to see how well they move and stay on their feet without losing balance," Coach Brad Banta of the Detroit Lions told me.

Wanting a few players' perspectives as well, I reached out to a few of my Trojan teammates, Rodney Peete, Matt Willig, and Pat Harlow who played 16, 14, and 8 years respectfully. They played for 12 different NFL organizations and have 38 years of combined NFL experience. As teammates of mine at USC, they witnessed and experienced what the weekly hitting was like, the individual drills, and the live scrimmages.

Seeking their opinions, I asked them to compare and contrast the average Division I college practice week versus the NFL practice week. Not surprisingly, they all had virtually the same answers and routine in the NFL. There was very little hitting during practice in the NFL, while in college, it was all out, smash-mouth football, typically two days a week and sometimes three.

Willig describes the NFL practice week as being all about learning and running through assignments rather than hard hitting. The lack of hitting during the week gave the NFL players time to get healthy and stay clear of injuries. Willig attests that the NFL practice schedule was nothing compared to college. While he dreaded the college days of practice, he enjoyed the "easy" days of the NFL practice schedule.

Quarterbacks are almost always off limits in practice and usually wear a red or yellow jersey that means "Don't Touch Me!" That is pretty universal at most levels of football including high school. And when they are "live," there is usually a walk-on QB running for his life. You don’t hit the QB in practice, unless he is a walk-on or fourth string.

Rodney Peete was a quarterback and had the luxury of wearing the yellow jersey in practice. However, from Peete’s perspective, he remembers the college way of practice and watching the battles of full contact, all-out hitting going on all around him as he scrambled all over the field. He even felt bad for his teammates who essentially were driving themselves to total exhaustion in the beginning of the week.

Pat Harlow did say there was fierce hitting and collisions going on during pre-season. That’s when guys are trying to make the team, especially the free agents or the NFL’s version of walk-ons. Once the regular season started, the hitting settled down to only one practice per week. That was much more manageable as their bodies had time heal.

I truly can't remember how many times I felt my ears ringing, experienced blurry vision, and felt stingers in my neck after hits during daily practice. While the media talk about concussions of big-name players in the NFL, it is important to note that massive head trauma is sustained at the college level as well, and let’s not forget who is on the receiving end of many of those vicious hits on the “tackling dummies.”

Walk-on’s are human tackling dummies. They are cannon fodder for scholarship players to practice their craft. People forget that walk-ons are on the receiving end of most of the brutal hits in practice. When these jarring blows occur, coaches seem more interested in how well their scholarship players perform the block or tackle than they are about the health and well-being of the woozy walk-on who is often told to get up and do it again.

So while we are discussing head trauma, let's not forget that we should consider incorporating some better guidelines in practice to protect the head slamming and remember there is a brain inside the helmet of that walk-on tackling dummy.

***

# Chapter 14
# Take It to Make It

CTE and other brain-related issues are not the only source of injuries to leave irreparable damage to players. When the Seau report came out in January 2013, I thought long and hard about the amount of hitting between the two of us. In fact, I started reading stories about the lingering and often undiagnosed injuries so many athletes suffer, especially in collision sports like football, hockey, and rugby.

It was then that I realized I had buried all my injuries away in my subconscious and had chalked them up to the normal aftereffects of college football. Rarely, if ever, do I discuss my nagging aches, pains, and injuries that still affect me today. The football mentality is probably the reason so many athletes just live with the aftermath for the rest of their lives. Do you really want to wake up every morning and complain to your spouse how bad you feel or how much pain you're in? You just deal with it internally.

Since I was the walk-on fullback trying to prove to the world that I deserved to play on Saturday, I suppressed all my injuries. One of our new USC team trainers was Paddy Jarit, and he and I became close. He was new to the team and still getting a feel for the organization. I felt like an outsider and would only go to Paddy to discuss my aches and pains. He knew I would not go to the team doctor or the head trainer because that would put me on the "Injury Report." I wanted to stay out of the training room and the injury news headlines. So I would seek out Paddy on the practice field and hint around as to what the heck was wrong with my body.

Both of my shoulders would routinely suffer a partial dislocation during practice drills or scrimmages. My shoulder would pop out of its socket and pop right back in. The pain was excruciating. Paddy diagnosed this on the field as a "subluxation." When one of my shoulders subluxed, I would drop to my knees in agonizing pain. It shot through my body like an electrical volt. However, I would gingerly jog back to the huddle doing my best acting job to show no signs of pain. I did not want to be taken out of the scrimmage or put on some injury report.

I did have to see Paddy or the team doctor after practice in the training room, but I downplayed the severity of the pain. Once we diagnosed the nature of the injury, I knew I could play through the pain so I kept my mouth shut after that every time it occurred. I would guess it happened to both shoulders more than 20 times apiece. When it did, I froze for a second, cringed, and went back to the huddle.

I had to take it to make it. I had to take the pain to stay on the field to prove I could play. Opportunities are few and far between for walk-ons. Your shot might come out of nowhere right in the middle of practice when a scholarship player gets dinged up. Therefore, it is always in the back of the walk-on's mind to never let the coaches see that you're hurt. Of course, you have to know the difference between pain and injury. You have to know what you can play through and what you can't.

For me, even though pain was shooting through my shoulder, I could still keep my hands down low and in front of my chest to make a block on the next play. If my assignment was to run into the flat on a pass pattern, I would just pray that the QB would not throw the ball high as there would be no way for me to lift my arms over my head to catch it. Fighting through the pain was a choice I made and the chance I took to play.

To this day, pain courses through my shoulders when I raise my arms above my head at a certain angle. When I sit too long I will get a sharp, shooting pain just to the right of my spinal cord in between my shoulder blades or a stiff, dull pain in my lower back. I lost most of the feeling in my left thigh just above my knee where there is about a five or six-inch diameter area I cannot feel.

When I was experiencing the effect of one of those ferocious hits from Seau, or one of the other defensive players, I should have walked to the sidelines to take off a play—or two. That would have been the logical and rational thing to do. As a walk-on, however, you feel you can't do that. You feel you have to prove you can "take it." If you show you can take the punishment and turn around and dish it back out on the next play, then maybe you can prove to the coaches that you can "make it." You have to show you can play with the big boys, the scholarship boys.

***

# Chapter 15

# Fraternity Brothers of Walk-On U

One would think that being named an All-State Linebacker and a finalist for the Mr. Football Award (the best high school football player in the state of Tennessee) would be a shoo-in for a scholarship to any Division I football program in the country. Apparently, that is not the case if you are 5' 9." Nick Reveiz was one of the best high school football players in the state. Yet his height was a concern for college scouts, who had little faith he would be successful playing NCAA Division I football. As a result, no scholarship offers were made to Nick.

Since his father, Faud Reveiz, played at Tennessee and had an 11-year NFL career as a kicker, and his uncle, Carlos, also played football at Tennessee, it was pretty much the clear choice that if Nick had to walk-on he would do so at the University of Tennessee. In 2006, Nick walked-on and became a Volunteer.

He entered fall camp in August 2006, and overnight he went from Mr. Football finalist to Mr. Nobody. Life was totally different for the new guys coming in, especially the walk-ons. Nick did not receive the newest equipment; he did not have an official number. He was not listed in the actual team roster. The team's media guide only listed his name, position, and high school in one line of text. That was it. There was no mention of his scores of awards and accomplishments from his high school days. However, the scholarship players had their photographs and a full bio of every great thing they had done since birth.

The wake-up call for this walk-on began to unfold for Nick. He hit the field realizing he would have to do everything he could to prove that he belonged on the team. Once the pads were strapped on, it was time to prove himself. He practiced with reckless abandon, which caused fight after fight with the older scholarship players not interested in going 100 percent on every play. They were not quite ready for Nick's overzealous attitude. Nick thought his aggressive style was catching the eyes of the staff, but they routinely ignored him.

He began to wonder if he would ever have a shot at playing in the games. His gut feeling was telling him, "No, you're just a walk-on!" It burned him up inside so badly that he would call his father nightly in tears.

Heaven forbid he go all out, full speed, and hit hard. The fights were on, and they were daily; scout team walk-on linebacker versus the starting offensive line. Nick went at it so hard that even a coach verbally unleashed on him one day. A day he will never forget.

After more than two months of playing on scout team and going all out, Nick was hoping he was getting noticed by the coaches. He was, except not every coach had a favorable opinion. One coach was getting so frustrated at Nick's going so hard that he stopped practice and scolded him for going 100 percent on every play. He told him bluntly to tone it down. He screamed at Nick saying he was going to hurt himself and that the O-Linemen could really hurt Nick if they went all out too.

That experience caught him so off guard that it affected him emotionally. When practice ended, Nick retreated to the locker room and found solace in the only place he could be alone. In full uniform, he went into a bathroom stall and fell to the ground in tears. He cried until nothing was left inside. Everything he had ever been taught about playing tough football and proving himself seemed to be falling apart and taken away from him. His feelings were that he would never play because he was a walk-on. If he practiced soft, he knew he would not get the attention of the coaches to play on Saturdays. If he went too hard, he risked upsetting his teammates and some coaches.

Nick's relentless battle on the field to make a name for himself was at the forefront of his priorities. It was part of his daily grind. Even when he did try and put football behind him, at least for an evening, he faced further challenges because of his walk-on status. He would try and blow off some steam and attempt to socialize with his new friends at the Saturday night parties. Of course, on the field he endured the everyday frustrations during practice of trying to prove he was somebody. However, he never thought that off the field he would be faced with questions at the weekend get-togethers as well.

When he did speak to new people, especially a girl he thought he wanted to get to know, she inevitably would ask what his football number was. When she looked him up, his name wasn't listed on the football team roster. Another player had that number, a scholarship player. Reveiz had not earned his spot on the roster yet. He and the other walk-ons were still in limbo land, trying to find their identity—and a number—they could call their own. They just wanted to be listed on the team roster for all to see.

Nick was trying to blend in with other students on Saturday nights and maybe meet a nice girl. But when he did, he would eventually be called out as the guy with no number. It was humiliating and dehumanizing. It became embarrassing for him to say he was on the football team because he feared being cut off at the knees. Who knew being a walk-on could make you go from a high school star to a college bum. Incredibly humbling.

In 2007, his second season, things were looking up. His perseverance was paying off, and things were falling into place. He earned a starting spot on all the special teams and made the travel squad. It was virtually unheard of for a redshirt freshman walk-on to be placed on every special team and make the travel squad, but he did it! He also was the leader in special team tackles with 15. Life was finally moving in the right direction, and there was a light showing at the end of the tunnel. A nice long career was on the horizon. Nothing could go wrong now, or so he thought.

Surely he was ready for the uphill battle to earn a starting spot at linebacker. That was his next goal, to play linebacker in games, not just special teams. What he didn't realize was that he was going to have to confront this challenge while dealing with family emergencies. Two events rocked his world, and no amount of weight lifting could help. He would have to rely on faith and medicine.

## The Day the Tumor Died

Nick's brother, Shane, a year younger, followed in his footsteps by walking-on at Tennessee in August 2007; two brothers playing on the same football team in college. Both were walk-ons fighting for everything they could get; together, they competed on the field until December of 2007 when a cardiogram brought results that Shane had been diagnosed with a life-threatening heart tumor. A new battle loomed for the Reveiz family.

Nick was supposed to be focusing on preparing for the

January 1st Outback Bowl against Wisconsin, but his mind was on his brother and prayer. Faith had entered his life like never before. He was praying for his brother's life. An open-heart surgery was scheduled for January 9, 2008, and the Reveiz family prayed.

Nick would have to play in the Outback Bowl with the uncertainty of his brother's life hanging in the balance. Nick played his heart out and he inspired his team to a 21–17 win over Wisconsin. There was little time to celebrate. Shane's life was still on the line.

Eight days later, Shane went under the knife. The surgery was a smashing success, and the growth on Shane's heart was successfully removed. Had the tumor not been removed for another three-to-four months, the doctors said he probably would not be with us today. A great victory was won that day; the day the tumor died.

Prayers were answered. Nick's faith had become the focal point of his life. Not only was Shane going to be fine, but the doctors gave him the thumbs up to play football again. Nick and Shane would be suiting up to play football together again in the fall of 2008. Nick dropped to his knees and thanked God. Nick now knew that anything could be taken from anyone at any moment so he continued to strengthen his faith and meet with other players who also had strong beliefs in the power above.

Spring ball started in March 2008, and Nick was determined to keep his starting spots on special teams and continue moving up the depth chart ladder at linebacker.

With two days before the final spring game in April 2008, Nick's faith was tested again. His sister, Bryanna, was involved in an auto accident on her way to school. She was airlifted by helicopter to the hospital in critical condition. This was a family's worst nightmare. The Reveiz family was rocked again. For the second time in just four months they were now praying for the life of another family member.

Nick, Shane, and their parents, Faud and Gayle, were at Bryanna's bedside within minutes. Bryanna shattered so many bones in her face and body that it would take 12 surgeries to put her back together. Because of Shane's heart issue, he was sitting out spring practice. But for Nick, the last two practices (Thursday and Friday) and the Orange and White Spring Football Game on Saturday were the most important days for Nick who was still battling it out for a top spot at linebacker.

However, sitting in the hospital that Thursday morning, Nick had all but forgotten about football. All he planned to do was to stay with his sister and pray. But somehow, someway, Bryanna had enough strength to gaze up at her brother. Behind a bandaged face, a broken jaw, and dried blood still in her hair, she managed to tell her brother, "Go to practice, I will make it."

As a family they prayed. After talking with his parents and the doctors, Nick was encouraged to go back to school for the afternoon practice, one of the hardest things he ever had to do.

On Saturday's final scrimmage, the Orange and White Game, Nick was second on the team in tackles with seven. He had finished spring ball the way he had hoped and the way he had prayed for it to happen. He then went back to the hospital to be with his sister. That Saturday evening was Bryanna's high school prom. Since she was stuck in a hospital, her girlfriends came to her bedside. Before they headed out for the big night, all her friends decked out in their prom dresses, came to see Bryanna. Her friends prayed for her.

Nick Reveiz once thought that football was the most important thing in the world. When he realized life happens in a flash and that things beyond his control could happen at any moment, he refocused his priorities and his faith took center stage.

As for Shane, he made a full recovery and went back to the Volunteers football team to vie for a starting linebacker spot.

And Bryanna? Well, God was good to her too. She made a full recovery, graduated from high school, and matriculated to UT where she watched her two brothers on the field from the student section cheering them on both as family and fellow undergraduates at the University of Tennessee.

After another stellar year on special teams in 2008, Nick was tied for most tackles with 10 and even got his feet wet starting one game at linebacker. His performance and inspiration set the stage for the 2009 season, and Nick was granted a full football scholarship!

Unfortunately, after 17 years at the helm, Head Coach Phillip Fulmer was going to step down after the 2008 season which would bring in a totally different staff. All the work Nick had done the last three years was out the window. He would have to prove himself all over again and show the new coaching staff who he was.

Lane Kiffin was named new head coach for the 2009 season and appointed his father, Monte Kiffin, to run the defense and the linebacker corps. Nick would have to prove to the new staff his scholarship was not granted because of his positive attitude and big heart. He had to prove he could play. When judgment day came, Monte Kiffin told his son and head coach Lane, that Nick Reveiz was going to be his starter.

Now a redshirt junior, Nick Reveiz was entering the season as the starting linebacker. But more importantly, Nick's teammates recognized his accomplishments by naming him team captain. The last time a walk-on had been named team captain by his teammates was in 1992. Now, 17 years later, fellow teammates bonded together to point to their new leader; the former walk-on turned worthy player, turned special-teams star, turned scholarship winner, turned starting linebacker, turned Team Captain!

Tragically, four games into the season Nick blew out his knee. He was leading the team in tackles with 27 when the injury occurred. He would spend the rest of the season on the injured list and did nothing but rehab.

Shortly after the 2009 season ended, Head Coach Lane Kiffin accepted the same position at USC. The departure of Kiffin opened the door again for a new coach and a new staff.

The Volunteers tapped Derek Dooley to be the new head coach for 2010. With every position up for grabs again, Nick would have to prove himself for the 153rd time. Nothing new for Reveiz; he would do it again!

As he entered his final senior season, Nick had fought his way back through the injury and once again earned back his starting spot at linebacker and retained the title of team captain via voting by his teammates.

Captain Reveiz had a great senior year and started every game at linebacker. Not surprisingly, Nick also led the team in total tackles with 94. He was listed as one of the top defenders in the SEC. What a career!

This walk-on is ready to show the world. In 2011, he got an invitation to training camp with the Tampa Bay Buccaneers but recently accepted a coaching job at Carson-Newman College where he is working with linebackers. Whatever the future holds for Nick Reveiz, there is no question he will be wildly successful. This young man can take on anything and conquer it. He is an inspiration. Even though I have never met Nick, I am proud to call him my w*alk-on fraternity brother*.

***

# Chapter 16
# Kickin' It

How does a high school senior boot a whopping three of six field goals (missing the three shortest ones), chip in just 4 of 7 extra points for the entire season and then walk-on to the University of Washington? How does that walk-on join the team as a punter and move to field goal kicker just before the first game his freshman year and become a four-year starter setting and smashing records along the way? How does that former walk-on become an All-American, get drafted into the NFL and have a 13-year professional career setting more records? *Belief*!

Jeff Jaeger did not have a stellar high-school kicking career to brag about. He was a good athlete and participated in football, baseball, wrestling, and track and field. But an athletic scholarship was certainly not in the cards. He was the football team's punter and he knew if he walked-on in college, his best bet would be as a punter.

During the high school signing period of February 1983, Jeff Jaeger spoke to the coaching staff at the University of Washington about the possibility of walking-on as a punter. He had already been accepted academically to the school so he made his plea to the coaches, and they welcomed his request. But at the same time the Husky staff was busy and focused on the scholarship athletes they were recruiting. Jaeger's walk-on status was not very high on their list of priorities.

As training camp approached, Jaeger had heard nothing from the staff and realized he had to politely remind the coaches of their agreement for him to walk-on. Then he had to gently beg to be allowed to enter training camp in August, rather than the typical "walk-on report date" of September when the school year started.

Reporting in August would give Jaeger the time and opportunity he needed to alter his destiny. While punting in camp, he learned that UW's expected kicker, an All-American Junior College transfer, quit after spring football camp. The other kicker in line was not performing as expected, and Jaeger was asked by the kicking coach to try some field goals; he did, and magic started to happen.

The key was the tee. In high school, Jaeger kicked off a 2-inch high tee for his field goals. In college a 1-inch high tee was used, and things began to click. He realized he was kicking further and more accurately. Rather than popping the ball up high in the air with less distance, he now had more control, distance, and accuracy. As his leg and foot got used to the new position and the slightly different angle he was kicking from, it all started to come together. His confidence started to soar and so did the belief in his own abilities. Jeff Jaeger got on a roll, won the job, and started from game one his true freshman year.

The Husky locker room did not have enough space for every player in the main room so the walk-ons had to dress in a separate, adjacent locker room. Head Coach Don James knew that must have made them feel a little isolated so he made sure to come into the walk-on locker room before every game and shake the hands of those players, calling them by their name. It was just a little something Coach James did to make the walk-ons feel like part of the team. That little gesture by Coach James went a long way in having the walk-ons feel welcome and needed, even though they were resigned to another locker room.

After the first three games his freshman year as the starting kicker, Jaeger was moved to the main locker room. The other walk-ons were ecstatic for him. The camaraderie the walk-ons had for one another was strong and they rooted for each other's success. Even though Jaeger got moved out of the walk-on room, his brothers cheered for him after the locker room promotion; they were proud.

Jaeger spoke of that special bond walk-ons have that no one else feels or understands. "We're going after the same thing, the opportunity to play, to prove ourselves. When one guy gets the chance or an upgrade in his status, there is no jealousy. Instead, there is an internal, and sometimes private, celebration within the walk-on club."

His performance during his freshman year earned him a full scholarship for the next three seasons. In his freshman and sophomore seasons, Jaeger was an Associated Press (AP) All-America Honorable Mention selection. As a junior, he received Second Team All-American honors by Football News, and in his senior campaign he became a consensus First Team All-American by United Press International (UPI) and the AP. He started every game all four years and set several records that stood for decades. Some still stand today. Jaeger is still the all-time Washington Husky scoring leader with 358 points and was inducted into the Husky Hall of Fame in 2004.

The Cleveland Browns selected Jaeger in the third round with the eighty-second overall pick of the 1987 NFL Draft. In his rookie season, Jaeger broke all of the Browns' rookie scoring records with 75 points despite playing in only 10 games.

He then moved on to the Raiders, and he was voted to his first Pro Bowl in 1991. He tied the Raiders' franchise record for the longest field goal with a 54-yard kick in 1992. In 1993, he led the NFL in scoring and set a new Raiders record with 132 points. That same year, he also led the NFL in completed field goals and tied the all-time NFL mark for field goal attempts. During a game against the Denver Broncos, Jaeger kicked a 53-yard field goal to win the game. Jaeger led the Raiders in scoring during five consecutive seasons and consistently ranked among the league's top 10 in scoring.

After his retirement from football at age 35, Jaeger traded his kicking shoe in for a real estate license and is extremely successful selling homes in Washington at jeffjaegerhomes.com. He credits his success in football and real estate to having that walk-on attitude and desire to excel and believe in himself. It was that belief that catapulted him from a UW walk-on kicker out of Kent-Meridian High School to receive All-American recognition honors in all four years as a Husky and a 13-year professional football career.

***

# Chapter 17
# Missing Man

An interesting trio created the battery for the PAT (point after touchdown) and FG (Field Goal) unit for the USC Trojans in 2006. In baseball the battery refers to the pitcher and catcher combination. I will take the liberty to call the long snapper, the holder, and the kicker the battery for the PAT/FG Team. This battery consisted of three walk-ons who all earned scholarships under Head Coach Pete Carroll.

Long snapper Will Collins walked-on in 2003 and earned the starting Long Snapper position the following year along with a scholarship. Mike McDonald also walked-on in 2003 and by 2006 he was the favorite holder earning him the starting nod and his own scholarship. Mario Danelo, also a 2003 walk-on, took over the duties as PAT and Field Goal kicker in 2005 and also graduated to scholarship status.

Throughout the 2005 season, the Trojans' powerful offense put the ball in the end zone or the red zone repeatedly giving the PAT/FG kicker plenty of opportunities to put points on the board. In doing so, Danelo set NCAA, Pac-10 and USC scoring records.

The battery of Collins, McDonald, and Danelo hit the 2006 season with a bang. Three walk-ons from the 2003 team had now all earned scholarships in their own right and were ready for another great year. Thirteen games later, Danelo had once again led the team in scoring and kicked two field goals in the Rose Bowl on January 1st, 2007 to help the Trojans earn the victory over Michigan to cap off another great season and a # 4 BCS National Ranking.

Sadly, six days after the Rose Bowl game, on January 7, 2007, Mario Danelo was found dead at the bottom of a 120 foot cliff near his home in San Pedro, California. He apparently slipped and fell to his death.

The funeral was held five days later. As a member of the Trojan Football Alumni Club Executive Board, I attended the funeral. What I witnessed that day captivated me. I told the president of our club what happened and he asked me to write it down so we could share it with our club board members.

I had not known Mario was a walk-on until the day of the funeral. I was shocked. He was so good. I was so proud. Every time I hear about a guy who "was" a walk-on, I get goose-bumps and obviously have a special feeling for those guys in my heart.

I wrote about my experience at the funeral and emailed it to a handful of guys in the club. Within 24 hours I started receiving emails from people I did not know. Within 48 hours I was receiving emails from people on the east coast. Within a week I had received emails from people in Australia and Hong Kong. It was amazing. Those two dozen or so men on the Trojan Football Alumni Club Board emailed my letter to family and friends and the power of the Internet took over. For the next five or six weeks I routinely received emails from people all over the world. It was one of the most fascinating experiences I have ever been a part of. I was asked for permission to have the letter published on Trojan web sites, magazines and later in a book titled; "What It Means to be a Trojan" by Steven Travers.

Here is the letter I wrote about my fellow walk-on brother:

## *Trojan in the Sky*

***Mario Danelo # 19 PK · USC Trojans Football · 2003-2006***
***12 January 2007***

*Today, I attended the funeral services of a young man I did not know personally, yet we are part of the same family; the* ***Trojan Football Alumni*** *family. Today, I witnessed families, friends and teammates coming together to pay tribute to a young man who touched the lives of thousands of people. I was not planning on writing about my experience but was inspired to do so.*

*When I got to the San Pedro church, there was a crowd of hundreds, maybe over 1,000 people gathered around the front entrance spilling on to the blocked-off streets. All roads surrounding Mary Star of the Sea Catholic Church were barricaded by the police department.*

*At 10:30 am, the casket, flanked by eight young men in the prime of their lives, was carried from the hearse, parked directly in front of the church, up the steps to the front doors. With over 100 USC football players and coaches in coat and tie surrounding the front of the church, they slowly followed the casket in a procession that proceeded inside and down the center aisle to the altar.*

*From the outside looking in, a funnel of ominous young men disappeared into the wide open doors that welcomed their entrance. Swallowed up by the flow of their wake, patrons began to file in side by side.*

*Mary Star seats some 1,500 people. Its high ceilings cast the sun light through scores of stained glass windows. The pews are split down the center with a wide middle aisle. Three quarters of the way down the center aisle is a cross aisle, creating a "t" or a "cross", if you will. With standing room only, both of the side aisles were jam-packed, making the cross aisle completely full, and the center aisle filled up. When it was time for the crowd to sit down, those that couldn't inadvertently created a standing human cross.*

*In the rear of the church, the vestibule was shoulder to shoulder, chest to back, twenty people deep. People continued to arrive only to find out there was no place left inside. Hundreds of mourners remained standing on the steps outside the church, spilling on to the sidewalk and into the street between parked limousines and police motorcycles. They were forced to listen to the outside loud speaker of what was being said on the inside.*

*Mario Danelo was just 21 years old when he left this earth six days ago. He was the place kicker for the USC Trojans. When officials cleaned out his locker, amidst the socks, cleats, t-shirts and shorts, was Mario's Bible. That Bible lay on top of his casket during the entire service.*

*During the homily, the priest spoke of doing mass services for the Trojan football team before games. He spoke of the tough loss at the end of the regular season being a tragedy. And then later, on January 1st, the victorious Rose Bowl game that turned into glory.*

*He spoke of the tragedy last week that took Mario away from us here on earth. And then, the victorious ascension into heaven that has turned into glory. And he spoke of remembering the great big smile on Mario Danelo's face.*

*When the mass had ended, four people got up to face the overflowing congregation, inside and out of more than 2,500 people.*

*First to speak was Joey Danelo, Mario's older brother. For some ten minutes, Joey captivated us with moments of sadness along with outbreaks of laughter. Fighting back the tears, he actually told several humorous stories of Mario's aggressive behavior from his childhood days.*

*He said Mario was the first 5–year-old basketball player to foul out of a game in the first 11 seconds of the first quarter. Later on, in little league baseball, he was the first pitcher to hit four batters in the same inning. Regardless of what he and his brothers did together, they were constantly having fun, living the life, and always smiling.*

*Joey said that Mario once told him you can tell the content of a man's character by how many people attend his funeral. He looked up from his written script to glance around the church through his watery eyes. It was beyond a chilling moment.*

*As they got older, they became even closer. In the past couple of years, they hung out with each other's friends and became even tighter. Joey finished his eulogy by saying, "Thank you, I love you buddy," and walked over and gave his brother one last little pat on the shoulder as his hand came down on the casket.*

*Brian, his friend of 20 years, took the podium. He too had several stories that created moments of laughter and sadness at the same time. Whatever happened while they were growing up, he could always remember Mario laughing and smiling.*

*Next to speak was from Mario's San Pedro High School football team, Coach Walsh. During the coaches' 26 year reign at the school, only three players were ever named to the All-Academic Scholar Athlete Team of Los Angeles, and Mario was one of them. On the field, he was an outstanding young football player who carried himself with grace, dignity and pride. Off the field, he was an exemplary student with the highest grades. On or off the field, Coach Walsh always saw Mario having fun, and always smiling.*

*Lastly, Coach Pete Carroll came to the microphone. He reiterated what the priest talked about earlier of this being a glorious day, and actually a time not to mourn Mario's passing but to celebrate his life. And oh man, how he did live. He was living the dream. Coach Carroll, not surprisingly talked of that "Mario Danelo smile" that we had heard so much about from all the others.*

*And then, for the first time in my life, I witnessed something that I had never experienced before at a funeral service. Coach Carroll talked about the NCAA scoring records that Mario has. He said "most of you don't know that Mario has the highest scoring record for college football. I think that is something to cheer about!" Carroll went on; "...now when I say Mario has the scoring record, I want to hear you!" Nervous laughter seemed to fill the church. And then Coach Carroll yelled out for all to hear; "MARIO IS THE SCORING RECORD HOLDER IN COLLEGE FOOTBALL!" The seated patrons rose to their feet in an eruption of thunderous applause, cheers, yelling, screaming and whistling. It was like being at the Coliseum and USC's Mario Danelo just kicked the winning field goal and the place is going wild!!!*

*For nearly two minutes the church was going berserk with deafening cheers on the inside, absolutely booming roars that filled the daytime sky on the outside and the entire building was shaking. People, blocks away, must have been thinking, "I thought there was a funeral going on at Mary Star????"*

*As the noise slowly started to subside, Carroll stepped away from the microphone, pointed at his 100 plus players in the front 15 rows and said, "COME ON, LET ME HEAR YOU!" The football players let out even loader cheers and cries that had to have echoed through the Coliseum Tunnel. The crowd went nuts again for another two minutes of constant clapping, cheering and whistling led by the Trojan team. It was one of the most amazing things I have ever seen.*

*Shortly thereafter, the priest gave his final blessing and the exodus of 2,000 plus began to overrun the streets and join those hundreds of others who had been out there for nearly two hours.*

*On my lapel I wore a* ***Trojan Football Alumni*** *pin. In my pocket, I had another lapel pin still in its package. I wanted the Danelo family to have it. But, not knowing them, it was certainly not appropriate for me to approach them at this time.*
*So, I wondered what to do as I stood on the grass on the side of the church. Not more than ten seconds elapsed when Coach Pete Carroll walked by, saw an opening on the sidewalk and stood alone only a few feet away from me.*
*Questioning my own thoughts of the right thing to do, I nervously approached Coach Carroll. With the pin in my hand, I reached out so he could see it. As he looked down at the pin in the palm of my hand, I said, "Coach, perhaps you can give this pin to Mario's parents. When Mario walked on the field, he was a Trojan Football Player. When he walked off the field for the last time, he became a Trojan Football Alumnus. He will always be part of the Trojan Football Alumni Club."*
*With that, Coach Carroll, took the pin out of my hand, looked me in the eyes and said, "Thank You. I will give it to them."*
*Today I witnessed what the Trojan Family is truly all about. Regardless if we know each other personally or not, we are always Family. You may not know us personally, but if you need us, we are here for you.*
*May God bless Mario, his family, friends, and teammates during this most difficult time.*
***FIGHT ON!***
***Tim Lavin***
***Trojan Football Alumni '88-'91***
***Club Secretary 2007***

**Back to Work**

The offseason was tough, but the Trojans had to get back to work. They did and they opened the 2007 season at home against the Idaho Vandals. However, what the players had planned for a tribute to Mario Danelo caught everyone off-guard. It was later voted by ESPN as one of the Top 10 Moments in the Pac-10 of 2007.

In the Air Force, at a funeral of a deceased pilot, a supreme tribute is sometimes paid. With military planes flying uniformly over the memorial, one peels off so that there is a missing plane in the formation to honor the fallen aviator. The missing man formation.

Former walk-on long snapper Will Collins came up with an idea and he asked his fellow former walk-on teammate and PAT holder Mike McDonald his thoughts. They suggested and requested that Coach Pete Carroll allow the PAT team to honor Mario after the first touchdown of the game. In the first quarter the Trojans scored a touchdown going up 6-0 and the PAT team entered the game. But, only 10 men hit the field.

In the players own version of the "Missing Man Formation," they lined up for the PAT with no kicker. Holder Mike McDonald waited for the lineman to get set. He put his fingers on the turf to mark the exact spot he would place the ball like he had done a thousand times before. He looked at the turf, he looked at his front nine teammates on the line of scrimmage, and then he looked back at the kicker. No one was there. Mike McDonald was looking at Mario, but no one in the LA Coliseum of 92,000 people could see him.

The PAT team froze in their position and waited. As the play clock slowly ticked down to zero, the crowd was now realizing the players' version of the Missing Man Formation in honor of Mario Danelo. The roars from 92,000 strong became deafening.

When the referee blew his whistle for the delay of game penalty, the squad huddled up as the new USC kicker, David Buehler, trotted onto the field. With 11 players now in their huddle the emotion was overwhelming and most players just stared at the ground with their eyes filled with tears. McDonald took control of the huddle. There was still a PAT to be kicked and a point to add to the scoreboard. He refocused the group and seconds later Buehler put the ball through the uprights for the extra point.

***

# Chapter 18

# The 12th Man According to "Law"

When you graduate high school with 35 students living in a town of 1,500 people, your life experiences are limited. The city of Tahoka, Texas, produced one of those students in Doug Lawson. Standing 6 feet 2 inches in the seventh grade, his future looked bright. His parents were a big influence on him, and his father taught Doug the lesson of discipline in out-working those around him. He started lifting weights and progressively grew into his big-framed body. By his freshman year, he was starting on the varsity football team. In fact, he was playing both offense and defense—he never left the field and played every down for four straight years.

Lawson was such a dominant force that he actually played just about every position on defense, lining up against the other teams' best players regardless of where they were on the field. The pros to that scheme allowed Lawson to play numerous positions, and he had a blast. The cons were that he could not concentrate or excel at one position leaving him with little exposure to the outside college recruiting world. Offensively, he played center on the O-line, which didn't exactly garner newspaper articles since centers don't usually get showered with press.

With no scholarship offers at the Division I or II levels, Lawson first went to Ranger Junior College for two years. Unfortunately, he was up against other star athletes and his Ranger JC years were nothing like high school. He never got the chance to play. But he excelled in the classroom and had the grades to enter any one of several major universities. In 1987, he selected Texas A&M because of their very strong network of alumni across the state. He also heard something about the *12th Man*.

Once at A&M, there was more talk of the 12th Man. In the early 1980s, Head Coach Jackie Sherrill started the tradition of the 12th Man Kickoff Team comprised of all eleven players being walk-ons for their home games. It was his way of engaging the student body (representing the 12th player). Intrigued and encouraged by his new friends, Doug went to the scheduled 12th Man tryout along with more than 300 other student-athletes. He made the first cut, then the next, and was ultimately asked by the staff to come try out again during spring practice. He did, and he made the team!

Exciting? Yes. But, at the same time, he felt like a nuisance. It was clear the equipment staff was not real high on the walk-ons. It seemed like just more clothes for them to wash and the pads he got were certainly not the most up-to-date in the equipment room. The trainers were not overly accommodating either when it came to taping the ankles of the walk-ons or giving them treatment for their bumps, bruises and other injuries. The excitement in being on the team was slightly overshadowed by the hierarchy and where the walk-ons had to dress … in a separate dressing area. They were not permitted to dress with their scholarship teammates in the main locker room.

Being a walk-on with school expenses, Lawson got a job. His first employment was washing dishes at the Student Health Center at 6 a.m. and 12 noon. By working these hours, Doug was able to eat breakfast and lunch for free before racing over to the football facility for the afternoon practice. The extra money he earned was used to pay for his training table dinner since walk-ons had to foot their own tab. Another job he had at the Student Health Center was in janitorial services. He cleaned the facility on weekends and holidays. It wasn't his dream job, but he did what he had to do.

Nevertheless, Lawson remained focused and determined to achieve his goal to play on Saturday, representing the student body as a member of the "12th Man Kickoff Team." To achieve his goal, Lawson prepared himself physically and mentally. He worked out hard in the weight room and on the practice field. Using mental imagery, he visualized running down the field in his assigned lane and reacting to the play as it developed.

After a year of preparation, he was knocking on the door to crack into the starting lineup of the $12^{th}$ Man squad when he pulled his hamstring. With the back of his leg black-and-blue and unable to walk, he had to rehabilitate his injury. But again, the training staff was focused on the scholarship players, and Lawson fell by the wayside. He was told where the ice machine was and where he could find bags for the ice, but that was about it. He would have to rehab himself back to health.

His passion to be part of the 12th Man Kickoff Team trumped his feelings regarding the lack of medical treatment he received—or did not receive. After nursing himself back to health, Lawson was ready to hit the field. On his first day back in pads at practice he was blindsided during a play and dislocated his shoulder. No!! He had just spent several months rehabilitating himself back to good health and now this. A member of the medical staff was kind enough to pop his shoulder back into place, but that is where it ended. Again, they pointed to the bags and the ice machine, gave him a list of exercises he might want to perform on his own, and Lawson began giving himself treatment all over again. When Lawson was ready to start practicing, the medical staff put Doug in a shoulder brace. It appeared to be one of the oldest and cheapest braces they had. It really didn't matter to Doug. He knew his hard work, passion, heart, and determination would carry him forward.

After many grueling months of rehab, the 1989 season rolled around and Doug Lawson stood poised and ready to make the kickoff team. At Texas A&M the 12th Man Kickoff Team was announced during pre-game introductions before the regular offensive and defensive starters. On that fall day when the 12th Man was announced, Doug Lawson's name echoed through the stadium as he hit the field. He was starting on the Kickoff Team.

That very moment lives in Lawson's memory as one of his most inspirational and unforgettable moments of his life. For it was during those precious moments of hearing his name over the loudspeaker to the roar of the home crowd that Doug realized that if you truly work hard enough and stick with it, never giving up, that you can basically accomplish anything.

This was such an incredibly important lesson for him to learn at such a critical time in his life. All the work he put in, the discipline, the never give-up attitude, the adversity he faced and dealt with, all paid off as he jogged onto the game field that afternoon. He would remember those principles for the rest of his life and use them more than he could ever imagine.

After his final practice in his senior year, he was walking off the field for the last time. As the sun was going down that late afternoon, he stopped, tuned around and looked at the field, his fellow teammates, the staff and all the memories that zoomed through his head. He thought for a moment about everything he had gone through and said to himself; "Yeah, it was all worth it."

He walked off the field for the last time proud of everything he had accomplished and experienced.

Because of his work experience during college, Doug believed he was destined to be in the health care industry and be part of something that really helped people. Within his first five years in health care, Doug landed a position as administrative coordinator for the cancer program at Scott and White Memorial Hospital and Clinic in Temple, Texas. Ironically, while working in the cancer program, Doug Lawson was diagnosed with Stage 4 Hodgkin's Disease which means the cancer cells had spread to his other organs. At 27, his will was tested once more, only this time it wasn't about whether he would run on a football field again, but whether he would live or die. And the very people he worked with were now caring for and treating him. He got to see life as a patient, giving him a totally different perspective…a priceless experience that would help him in his career.

Along with hearing his first diagnosis came the overwhelming, depressing feeling of *Oh my God, why me?* followed by, *I'm going to die!* Very quickly after that disheartening feeling, he made a decision to change his mindset to the other end of the spectrum. *No, I'm not going to die, I'm going to fight this and I'm going to win!* He needed to put a plan together. How was he going to fight this? What could he do to prepare his body for all the chemotherapy it was about to absorb?

He thought about what he did as a walk-on. His plan was to get focused and stay disciplined. He was passionate with all his heart, desire, and willingness to accomplish his new goal, to beat cancer. He got his mind set spiritually and mentally. He visualized his body beating the cancer. While some may argue that mental imagery is not an effective tool, Lawson contends that while it perhaps may not be an effective clinical tool, it is an effective emotional tool.

Lawson stayed with his plan and spent a year going through chemotherapy and all the nastiness that went with it. By year's end, the cancer went into remission, and Doug Lawson has been cancer free since 1995.

Because of the chemo he underwent, Doug knew that he probably could never have children. But the good news was that he beat the cancer. However, a decade after the cancer left his body, Doug and his loving, beautiful wife, Jennifer, gave birth to their own son, Jack. They call him their miracle baby.

Doug lived by those principles that carried him through A&M and fighting cancer. In doing so, he climbed the corporate ladder in dramatic fashion. He moved on to Senior Vice President at Cabell Huntington Hospital in West Virginia and then became President of Baylor Regional Medical Center. His incredibly successful performance as president led to a new challenge as Chief Operating Officer at Baylor University Medical Center. He is getting his PhD in Leadership Development to further make him the best he can be. And when people ask Doug about running a hospital, he can literally say his first job in health care was washing dishes and cleaning toilets.

Doug Lawson has come a long way. From his small town of 1,500 people, his graduating class of 35 students, his walk-on experience of trying out with 300 potential players and making the cuts, his separate dressing room, getting the oldest equipment, washing dishes at 6 a.m. for free food, fighting through injuries, learning to rehab himself, getting back on the field, going into the health care industry, getting married, moving up the corporate ladder, being diagnosed with a deadly disease, fighting back and becoming cancer free, becoming a senior vice president, then a president, having a miracle child, and now as chief operating officer … I know Lawson looks at his life's journey and says, "Yeah, it was all worth it."

***

# Chapter 19

# The One-Month Walk-On

Ben Graniello played offensive line at Coronado High School in El Paso, Texas. Like almost all high school athletes, he filled out scores of forms and questionnaires for colleges and universities around the country and played his heart out in that 1999 senior season. The February 2000 high school signing day came and went, but no scholarships were offered to Ben. Baylor University seemed interested in having Ben walk-on, but so did the school in his own backyard, University of Texas, El Paso. The school was also open to the idea of Ben walking-on, and UTEP Director of Football Operations Nate Poss had ties to Coronado High School where he had coached in the mid-1990s.

Poss told the UTEP O-line coach, Sean Kugler, about Graniello and the two paid a visit to Ben's home. They were interested in his walking-on the football team and they explained that Head Coach Gary Nord had a unique policy. He held two scholarships back each year and gave them to the most deserving walk-ons. Being brutally honest and straightforward, they made no guarantees and made sure Ben knew it could take a couple of years to earn the scholarship, and also that it might never happen. He would have to battle it out each year with all the other walk-ons on the team. After careful consideration, the decision was made that Ben would attend UTEP in hopes of one day being the walk-on who earned that scholarship.

Determined to get better, Ben sought permission from the UTEP coaching staff to attend the voluntary summer workout sessions, and his request was granted. He never missed a single day and worked his tail off in the weight room and in O-line drills with other UTEP players. Being part of the summer workouts had Ben's teammates treating him like one of the guys. He felt like part of the team. This was a huge physical and mental advantage for Ben going into two-a-day training camp in August. Even though Ben was an incoming freshman, he almost felt like a veteran since he had spent so much time training with the upper classmen during the summer.

For all of two-a-days in August Ben was rotated in with all the other linemen in their one-on-one drills and scrimmages. The time and dedication he spent in the summer workouts rendered his walk-on status almost inconsequential—that is until school started and training table became an issue.

For three weeks of training camp in August, Ben and the other walk-ons ate three square meals a day with their teammates. But once school started, the NCAA rules kicked in. They would now have to start paying approximately $12 a day for the privilege to dine with their teammates or go elsewhere to eat.

Although Ben was going to major in engineering, it did not take a math guru to figure out that $12 a day to eat at training table could add up quickly, especially on a tight, fixed budget. Ben was one of the walk-ons who realized he could eat someplace else for closer to $5 a day and get by. After a week of not eating with his teammates, he got tapped on the shoulder by Operations Director, Nate Poss. Ben was informed by Poss that Head Coach Nord wanted to see him in his office immediately. Although Poss knew exactly the reason he was summoned to retrieve the player, he asked Ben questions like; "Ben, what have you done? What did you do wrong?"

Ben was shaking. Butterflies fluttered through his stomach. His mind was racing, wondering what he did to get in trouble. He was petrified and entered the coach's office. In his trembling voice, Ben asked the coach why he wanted to see him. Coach Nord told Ben to take a seat. Palms sweating, Ben sunk into the chair.

Coach Nord told Ben he did a great job in the voluntary summer workouts and appreciated his dedication. He also told him that he had worked hard for the three weeks of training camp and into the first week of the season. The coach took a deep breath, paused, and then dropped it on him. "Ben, we've selected you as one of our walk-ons most deserving of a scholarship!" Ben doesn't remember what was said next. He just remembers being in a total state of shock. After practice later that afternoon, Coach Nord made the official announcement to the whole team. Ben's football brothers were elated and cheered loud and proud! Later that evening, Ben returned to training table with his teammates, where he remained for the next five years without concern for the $12 cover charge.

In just one official month of practice Ben Graniello had worked his way into scholarship status, an accomplishment very few walk-ons achieve, and those who do, often wait years. Ben's all-out hustle and dedication earned him that coveted award in just 30 days.

Ben's student loans were canceled and his first loan payment he had already paid was reimbursed when his scholarship kicked in shortly following that special meeting with Coach Nord. Ben not only graduated in four years with an engineering degree, but his scholarship also funded his master's degree at UTEP.

Graniello redshirted his first year (2000), traveled and played in a handful of games his freshman and sophomore years (2001-2002), started five games his junior year (2003), and was the starting right guard every game for his senior season (2004).

Ben credits his summer workouts at UTEP with the team prior to his freshman year as the best decision he ever made. He obviously took his school work very seriously as well, firmly believing in his personal mantra; *hard work and dedication go a long way.*

Today, Ben Graniello is an electrical engineer designing computer chips for Intel, and some of his business travel has taken him to Intel plants in many countries around the world.

***

# Chapter 20
# Walk-On Warrior

Brad Cousino was never wanted. His parents had to get married because she was pregnant at age 15. It was 1952. In Cousino's words, his dad was an alcoholic, and his mother was a rage-o-holic. The only ego-stroking he remembers occurred when he excelled in athletics. It was the 1960s in Toledo, Ohio, when a young man found himself entrenched in either working odd jobs to earn money or involved in sports, in particular; hockey, football, baseball, and wrestling. The reality was Cousino would do anything to keep himself focused on something other than spending time at home.

He recognized that he did get positive affirmation from his parents when he excelled in grade-school and high-school sports, but not so much when he didn't do well, the days he feared most. Always the underdog as one of the smaller kids, he had to utilize the intangibles he possessed to make a difference and not get lost in the shuffle. If he had a good day on the field, his parents were nicer to him than when he didn't. Without understanding why, it became his driving force.

His father worked at Libbey-Owens-Ford glass factory never making more than $11,000 a year. No one on either side of his family had ever gone to college. Brad Cousino could not bear to imagine a future working in a glass factory and became focused on finding a way to go to college. The only problem was his parents could not afford to send him. He felt his only hope was to earn a football scholarship.

Playing fullback and linebacker for Central Catholic High School in Toledo earned him All-League, City, and District Honors, but not quite All-State. Some recruiters seemed intrigued by his high-school performance until they got up close and personal. Standing 5 feet 11 ½ inches and 185 lbs., he was thought by scouts to be too small for major college football and was passed up on the recruiting trail.

Linebackers in those days were typically closer to 220–230 pounds. Even the immortalized coach, Woody Hayes, from Ohio State had heard this kid was good and paid him a visit. When Coach Hayes saw Cousino in person he inadvertently laughed when he observed his frame and explained that, at 185 pounds, he would never play college football. Coach Hayes walked out the front door faster than when he walked in. It was a crushing blow to a boy's hopes and dreams.

Unfortunately, Coach Hayes' remarks seemed to ring true as Brad Cousino was not offered any scholarships by any school. In March 1971, his senior year in high school, Cousino wrestled with the fact that he had been overlooked by every Division I, II, and III college and university within 200 miles of Toledo. Every school in the Big 10 and the Mid-American Conference (MAC) including (Ohio State, Michigan, Bowling Green, and Toledo) looked elsewhere for talent. Knowing his parents were broke and there was no way he could go to college without a scholarship, Cousino took a trip by himself to Miami University (MAC Conference) in Oxford, Ohio, and begged the coaches for a scholarship. He knew an older high school classmate who went to play football at Miami U and used that as his excuse to tell his parents, so he could drive 200 miles to see the coaching staff. While they liked his enthusiasm, they had no scholarships available, and Cousino was sent on his way.

Dejected, but not defeated, he wrote a letter to every MAC school and other D-I schools (even small colleges like Ashland College) that were anywhere close to Ohio. He heard nothing until a few weeks later when Bob Reublin, the assistant coach from Miami of Ohio, who recruited from the Toledo area, called. "Are you still interested in coming to Miami University?" Cousino jumped up; "YES! Do you have a scholarship available for me?" "Well, no but we would like to know if you would be willing to walk-on as a non-scholarship player." Cousino informed the coach that his parents could not afford the school. The coach told him that an alumnus of Miami U thought he could get Cousino a construction job in the Toledo area for the summer. It would be really tough, but if he was willing to do it, he could make enough money to pay for at least the first quarter of his tuition. Miami U was on a quarter system rather than the typical two-semester schedule. The coach asked, "Are you willing to do construction?" Cousino, of course, said "I'll do anything!" That summer Brad Cousino worked 25 feet underground in the storm sewers along Routes I-75 & I-475 picking up the sludge and garbage from all the sewer lines running through the city of Toledo while getting paid $5.25 an hour. With his miner's hat, a small wagon, and a scoop shovel, Cousino dredged through cesspools to keep a dream alive. It was the price he had to pay to earn enough so he could fund the first quarter of tuition at Miami of Ohio. Not knowing how he would pay for the second and third quarters that year, he would be praying and throwing fate to the wind.

Cousino entered training camp in August 1971 and was listed as third string linebacker on the freshmen team. Freshmen were not eligible to play on the varsity squad until 1972. Yet freshmen were also the scout team against the varsity team in practice every day. Being third on the depth chart left him with few opportunities to prove himself in practice. He just didn't get many chances to show what he could do. He needed a chance, an opening, a big break, something….

About three weeks into training camp, a fellow freshman who was a defensive lineman went AWOL. He had been starting at nose guard on the freshmen team and on scout team against the varsity. He was a big 250-pound bruiser and one day after the morning practice session he just packed his bags and left town. The varsity coaches did not even realize the guy wasn't in practice until they lined up for the scrimmage against the freshmen scout team later that day.

When the freshmen jumped in at their respective positions and lined up ready to go against the varsity, only 10 men hit the field. The nose guard position was vacant. A fate-altering opportunity was born. Within seconds, Brad Cousino saw and seized a moment that would change his life forever. Cousino sprinted onto the field and lined up in the defensive lineman position. The coaches screamed at the now 193-pound walk-on; "Cousino get out of there! You're too small. You'll get killed. Get off the field!" In what many would describe as a slow-motion moment, Cousino turned around, pointed at the coach and screamed back, "*I CAN DO IT*!" He put his fingers back down in the turf and dug his cleats in the grass ready for battle.

Shaking their heads in disbelief and not wanting to waste more practice time, the coaches ran the play. Brad Cousino DOMINATED! Shocked with what they were witnessing play after play, the coaches let Cousino stay in at nose guard. By the end of the afternoon, he had made so many tackles that the coach made the varsity offensive linemen run extra wind sprints after practice. You can only imagine how well received Cousino was by his varsity teammates! They wanted to kill the walk-on rookie freshman nose guard who was but a mere 193 pounds.

After that practice, the freshmen coaches officially moved Cousino from linebacker to defensive middle guard where he started on the freshmen team and earned Most Valuable Player of the Defense for the freshmen team that season. As a result of his outstanding performance, Cousino's grandfather stepped up and paid for his second quarter tuition. Shortly thereafter Miami U came up with a 1/3 scholarship to pay for Cousino's third and final quarter that year.

Going into spring football camp, Cousino was listed as third-string on the varsity team. By the time spring ball had ended, Cousino had won the starting spot and was rewarded with a full scholarship for his next three years. Rolling the dice on a dream, his prayers were answered.

He started every game his sophomore season and continued to dominate despite not weighing more than 197 pounds. The team finished 7-3. Also in 1972, a player by the name of Jack Lambert, a junior from Kent State, won the MAC Defensive Player of the Year Award. Lambert, as you may remember, went on to become one of the most prolific linebackers in both Pittsburgh Steelers and NFL history winning four Super Bowls and being named to Pro Football's Hall of Fame in 1990.

However, in Brad Cousino's 1973 junior season (Jack Lambert's senior year), the former walk-on out-hustled, out-worked, and out-played the entire conference averaging a daunting 20.5 tackles per game. Cousino was named the MAC Defensive Player of the Year, beating out Jack Lambert. The Miami Redskins (now called the RedHawks) finished the season 11-0 by beating Florida on its home field in the Tangerine Bowl and ended up being ranked fifteenth in the country in the Associated Press (AP) Poll.

Not surprisingly, he would do virtually the exact same thing in his 1974 senior season averaging 19.5 tackles per game and was awarded the MAC Defensive Player of the Year for the second year in a row. He was named to the All-American Team and the Redskins finished the season 10-0-1 by beating Georgia in the Tangerine Bowl and were ranked #10 in the country in both the AP and Coaches Polls.

Interestingly, sports writers and coaches who selected Cousino for the 1974 All-American Team listed him as a linebacker because they felt no one would believe an All-American defensive lineman could weigh less than 200 pounds and be that dominating. So, he was awarded First Team All-American as a *linebacker* and not for his actual position of nose guard despite never playing a single down at linebacker in college.

The NFL seemed to have the same mindset as college scouts when it came to size over a player's ability. As a result, Cousino was passed up in the NFL draft back when they had 17 rounds and a total of 442 picks. Even two Division I *basketball* stars were drafted due to their size though they never played a single down of football in college. No one was interested in the 198-pound nose guard even with his incredible stats. However, Hall of Fame Legend, Coach Paul Brown of the Cincinnati Bengals, (a Miami U Alumnus) followed schools in the Ohio region and saw Cousino's name in the paper so much that he called him after the NFL draft and said he would bring him in to training camp as a non-drafted free agent if—and only if—he could come in at 218 pounds.

Always having had trouble gaining weight throughout college, Cousino would now have to gain 20 pounds in a very short period. He heard of a new weight lifting program just hitting the scene called Nautilus and became part of an intensive eight-week training program to test its value that was being conducted at the United States Military Academy at West Point. All Cousino did was eat and work out. When the Bengals camp opened up, Cousino reported in at 218 pounds, and he was allowed by Coach Brown to stay in camp and try out.

He never played a down at linebacker in college but was listed as the number 12 linebacker in the 1975 Bengal's training camp. There were seven returning linebackers from the previous year and four linebackers who were picked in the '75 NFL Draft. Cousino was listed behind all of them. The Bengals would keep only six or seven linebackers for the season. Most of Cousino's opportunities in camp came as a scout team player, but he was given the opportunity in pre-season games on the special teams. Cousino was in on 65 percent of the tackles in those games and on sheer grit and desire, Cousino made the team.

He spent his first NFL season with the Bengals, his second season with the New York Giants, and his third with the Pittsburgh Steelers. In his fourth and final season, he went to the Toronto Argonauts of the Canadian Football League before ending his professional playing career.

Brad Cousino had that special gene, an inherent quality that relishes the challenge when he ever heard the word *no* and would do whatever it took to prove others wrong and himself right. He lives by the motto: *you can do what you want if you are willing to pay the price*. He adds; "I've been blessed with a passion to encourage people to become much more than they realize, to get them to understand that they need to be willing to strive to reach their God-given potential and never quit on themselves. I know that you can accomplish *anything* if you are willing to never lose sight of your dream. I encourage everyone to go after their dream, with *passion*, hard work, and never doubt that you can do it if you are willing to pay the price. You will have success provided you just don't ever quit on your goal or dream. You always *win* if you never quit on yourself."

He talks about the little things that can change your life. Things you can control—your attitude, your willingness, and your heart. What about visiting a coach, writing a letter, working in a sewer, walking-on, or jumping in to play when a door opens ever so slightly? What if he never did any of those things? He would have missed out on an amazing chain of events that had far-reaching repercussions. He would not have met his wife of 35 years at Miami U and had the four children he has. He would never have gone to college. He might still be working in a glass factory.

Instead, he is a Senior Partner at The Mastery Team doing executive-level (www.TheMasteryTeam.com) coaching and consulting to small and midsize business owners on how to be more successful and passionate entrepreneurs. He now has broad experience in commercial real estate as an investor, developer, and property manager. He is the first person in his family to finish four years of college, was a two-time MAC Defensive Player of the Year Award winner, an All-American and an NFL veteran. All because he believed and bet on himself.

Cousino wasn't the tallest, fastest, biggest, or strongest. He was told *no* and *never* by people he knew and respected. But instead, he shocked and amazed his family, friends, recruiters, teammates, coaches, sports writers, and NFL gurus. How? Because he used the intangibles to find leverage to get the job done; and he believed in himself. He bet on himself when no one else would. Being a walk-on and facing the obstacles he had to overcome made him a better player. It also helped him realize that no matter your circumstances, you can change. You don't have to accept the fate of coming from a very dysfunctional home where yelling, cursing, and beatings were a way of life. As Cousino stated "I recognized that despite my upbringing, there is a good God who loves me, and as such I am a far better husband, father, papa, and human being than I would have been. And that is far more important than being just a good football player." Now there is a true **W**alk-**O**n **W**arrior, WOW!

***

# Chapter 21

# The Life Changing Game

It is considered one of the most exciting games in the storied USC/UCLA rivalry. It is arguably one of the greatest Bruin victories in the school's history. The 1992 game ended 38-37 over the heavily favored Trojans who were ranked 15$^{th}$ in the country at the time. The Bruins were down 31–17 when the fourth quarter started. Behind the great heroics of a walk-on QB who was originally fifth string on the depth chart, let me introduce you to the man behind the story—John Barnes.

The 1987 high school football season revealed a promising senior quarterback at Trabuco Hills High School in Orange County, California. John Barnes had the stats to prove he was worthy of playing at the next level. The only problem was that there was another quarterback in Orange County getting all the press. Todd Marinovich of Capistrano Valley High School was the most sought after high school quarterback in the country. His record-setting statistics had the attention of every school in the nation and of the press. Marinovich accepted a scholarship to USC. Any other year might have given Barnes the opportunity to be looked at by many universities. As it was, John Barnes received no scholarship offers and generated only a ripple of attention from some Division II schools.

He chose to go the two-year junior-college route as a stepping stone to a Division I program and enrolled at Saddleback JC. In his first year, he redshirted (practiced) and did not play in any games. In year two, Barnes took over the starting QB duties but did not perform up to his potential and ultimately lost his starting spot. Since his season at Saddleback was not up to par, there was no stone to step up onto via a scholarship at the Division I level.

It was now 1990, and legendary coach, George Allen, took the head coaching job at California State University, Long Beach. Barnes decided he would walk-on at Cal State Long Beach and be tutored by the great Coach Allen. John went to the equipment room and asked for a football so he could practice his mechanics. The equipment manager told Barnes; "We don't give footballs to walk-ons." John's gut feeling told him that if walk-ons were going to be treated this way, he didn't want any part of it, nor did he see any possibility of getting a chance to show his skills. A week after he enrolled at Cal State Long Beach, he un-enrolled.

Discouraged, but not giving up on his career as a football player, John wanted a change. He felt he needed to get out of California to take on new scenery, new players, and a new team in a new state. Somehow he chose Western Oregon State College as the place to start anew. As it turned out, Western Oregon State had their own quarterbacks and they were not too keen on the California kid coming in and taking over. They even tried to move John to tight end. Frustrated and knowing he could play quarterback, it was time to move on.

Next stop was the University of California Santa Barbara (UCSB). Barnes took the reins in 1991 and played lights-out football, throwing for over 2,100 yards and 23 touchdowns. John Barnes was not playing Division I, but he was playing quarterback and playing great.

When the UCSB Gauchos' season ended, Barnes decided to go to Los Angeles to visit his girlfriend and use her student ID to sneak into the LA Coliseum to watch the Trojans and Bruins battle it out. As Barnes sat in the famed old stadium that afternoon, his mind kept telling him he could play on that field, at that level. But he was the starting quarterback at UCSB, and that was where he was going to finish his last year. Or, so he thought.

A few months later UCSB dropped its entire football program, and Barnes' future was in limbo for the fourth time in four years. He sat on his couch pondering his life and football career. While reading the sports page one day, he saw that the UCLA quarterback, Tommy Maddox, had declared himself eligible for the NFL draft. The light bulb went on in John's head and he immediately thought back to the USC/UCLA game months earlier where he envisioned himself on the field playing in front of more than 90,000 people. With Maddox gone, maybe—just maybe there was a chance John could walk on at UCLA.

Barnes remembered that his old JC coach knew UCLA Head Coach, Terry Donahue, and called to see if he could arrange a meeting. It was set up, and Barnes headed to the Westwood campus for the introduction. John showed up in Coach Donahue's office wearing a three-piece suit and carrying a briefcase filled with his UCSB game tapes.

Coach Donahue thought John was an insurance salesman, while Receiver Coach, Rick Neuheisel, thought some kid from Wall Street was looking to interview for a job. After Barnes assured the coaches he was John Barnes, the quarterback from UCSB, looking to walk-on the UCLA football team, they viewed some of his game tape.

Interestingly, John's younger brother, Pat Barnes (a senior in high school), was at the same time being recruited by UCLA to come and play quarterback. Donahue said he saw a predicament with UCLA wanting to recruit Pat Barnes while older brother John was trying to walk-on and also play quarterback. Donahue told John straight up that he would probably never play a down if he did walk on. Barnes replied that UCLA might have a better chance at getting his younger brother if he too were on the team.

Intrigued, the coaches wanted to see what John could do so they went out to the practice field. Still in his three-piece suit and dress shoes, John took the ball and did several drop backs and throws to show what he had. The UCLA Bruins football team was also on the field working out. Of course they were in their shorts and t-shirts running around and laughing at the insurance salesman doing QB drills in his Sunday best.

His performance convinced the coaches to allow Barnes to walk-on, and Donahue said he needed about a week to confirm that John could transfer from UCSB to UCLA. Even though it was not a done-deal, John told his parents he had been accepted and not to pay his tuition at UCSB. He was transferring. John spent the next week living in his car and banking on the transfer going through. After dozens of Chinese takeout meals and driving around aimlessly while waiting for the news, John was finally notified he was accepted into UCLA.

Brother Pat later accepted a scholarship to the University of California, Berkeley, so there would be no brotherly QB rivalry at UCLA. There were five quarterbacks at the campus, and John was listed as the last one behind four scholarship players. Barnes participated very little in QB drills, having been told instead to just hold blocking dummies in practice.

During pre-season "two-a-days" in August, John ate by himself at team meals. No one seemed to want to socialize with the new walk-on who was in his last year of eligibility. He felt like a loner but kept his focus on playing. Every day he would ride his bike to class and pictured in his mind quarterbacks getting hurt and Terry Donahue calling on him to get in the game. He replayed that dream in his mind hundreds of times.

Also while riding on his bike; John created three goals for his final season of college football. The first goal was to get into a game. The second goal was to start a game. The third goal was to win a game. These were some lofty goals, especially after the head coach told him he would be getting very few reps in practice, let alone a near zero chance of ever getting in a game.

The 1992 season began, and starting-quarterback Wayne Cook suffered a season-ending injury in the first game. Still low on the depth chart, John Barnes started to get more reps in practice.

In the third game, the Bruins were beating San Diego State, and with just a handful of plays left in the game, Coach Donahue turned to Barnes on the sidelines and asked if he wanted to go in. Of course, Barnes jumped at the chance even though it was scrap time and he would just be handing the ball off a few times to end the game. He fulfilled his first goal with the thrill of playing on UCLA's home field in the Rose Bowl, if only for a few plays.

The next two games saw more injuries and poor play by the UCLA quarterbacks, and John Barnes was moving up the ladder and getting some playing time. By the sixth game of the season,

Barnes felt he had a chance at starting, and he also felt a new leader needed to emerge on a team that had lost their last two games. He wondered if he could be that leader. Would the team follow a walk-on into battle?

John had been watching Vietnam War movies at the time and had just seen John Irvin's 1987 film, *Hamburger Hill*. The movie shows how the American forces faced heavy casualties, including many from friendly fire. Nevertheless, the soldiers overcame the brutal conditions and fought their way to victory in the battle conquering Hamburger Hill.

The night before the Washington State game, Terry Donahue held their normal Friday night team meeting at the hotel. With two losses in the past two games, there was tension in the room. Everyone could feel it, and they heard it in the coach's voice. When Donahue was finished speaking, John unexpectedly stood up. Donahue was puzzled and looked to Barnes. "You have something to say, John?" Shaking, John turned to address his teammates.

Nervous because he might be laughed at for speaking up, John took a deep breath and started to tell a story—the story of Hamburger Hill. He compared the friendly fire that the American soldiers incurred to that of the UCLA offense and defense fighting each other during practice. He went on to compare the adversities American forces were faced with during the battle with the difficulties and misfortunes their football team had endured. And then, with great passion in his voice, he linked the Americans fighting back and conquering Hamburger Hill with UCLA's punishing Washington State on Saturday, grabbing the UCLA flag, and sticking it in the 50 yard line after the game! The team erupted into cheers and applause. John finally felt a surge of acceptance by his peers.

On Saturday, 20 minutes before kickoff, Coach Donahue put his arm around John and said, “How can I not start the guy who talked about Hamburger Hill?” John Barnes started that game accomplishing goal number two—to start a game.

Unfortunately, John was so pumped up that he threw an interception which was returned for a touchdown, and Donahue pulled Barnes after only the fourteenth play. Ryan Fien replaced Barnes and Fien never came out.

The Bruins lost the game, and Barnes thought he would never get a chance to play again. Coach Rick Neuheisel sat next to an emotional Barnes on the plane ride home to keep his spirits up. Neuheisel compared his own emotional rollercoaster experience when he was a walk-on quarterback at UCLA fighting with Steve Bono for the starting QB spot nine years earlier. Encouraged by the talk with Neuheisel, Barnes kept his focus.

While Barnes did not start the next game against Arizona State, he was put in the game in the fourth quarter when Coach

Donahue was looking for a spark to get his offense going. Barnes had been overloaded with the playbook. He had a crash course on learning the offense since he had spent most of the spring and much of the early days of fall so low on the depth chart. He now had to execute with precision and with very little preparation. He confided to Coach Neuheisel that he did not always know who he was supposed to read and throw to. Barnes asked, even begged, Neuheisel to give him some help. During the game, John would call the play, walk up to the line of scrimmage and look to the sidelines. Neuheisel would hand signal to Barnes which receiver he was supposed to throw to. They made up secret hand signals for the "X, Y, and Z" receivers. The hand signals were so secret, only Barnes and Neuheisel knew what was going on.

Coach Neuheisel told Barnes that if Head Coach Terry Donahue found out what the two of them were up to he would be fired. They made a Walk-On pact not to tell a soul. John Barnes did not tell anyone, not even his parents, for more than 10 years.

On a couple of occasions during the next few games, Barnes did not see or could not make out the quick hand signal Neuheisel flashed without Donahue seeing. One time, Barnes called a time-out. Coach Donahue was incensed. He screamed at Barnes on the sideline: "I'm the head coach, I call the time-outs!" Later in the game, Barnes nervously called another time-out. A ballistic Coach Donahue jumped in his quarterback's face: "If I had another healthy quarterback you would be out of here!" Barnes listened to Donahue ripping his ear off but, focused on Neuheisel standing close by to flash the hand signal he would need for the next called play.

Finally, the last game of the year against USC had arrived. Barnes was healthy and played well enough to be tapped as the starting QB against the fifteenth nationally ranked Trojans. This meant more to John than any other experience he had encountered during the year. It was incredibly surreal to him as he remembered sitting in the stands one year earlier as the starting quarterback for UCSB and watching the Bruins and Trojans battle it out at the LA Coliseum. He recalled thinking to himself, "I could do that!"

One year later, he was on the national stage at the Rose Bowl in Pasadena, Calif., playing in one of the biggest rivalry games in college football. It was Senior Day. Coach Donahue told the seniors before they hit the field to remember this day. John Barnes took it literally.

When the seniors were announced, John ran onto the field as 100,000 people cheered for him. He remembers that feeling as the most intense, exhilarating feeling in the world. John looked up into the huge crowd, and with tears in his eyes, he remembered his path from high school to that moment. He thought about his journey to Saddleback Junior College for two years, then a one week stop at Cal State Long Beach, then on to Western Oregon

State College for a year, then UC Santa Barbara for a year. He recalled watching this very game from the bleachers one year earlier. He thought about all the coaches along the way. Some believed in him, others did not. Now he was gazing up at the stands filled with 100,000 people, and he was the starting quarterback for UCLA.

The game got under way, and with the score tied at 10 in the middle of the second quarter, John Barnes hit JJ Stokes for a 57-yard touchdown pass to go up 17-10. The Trojans followed with a touchdown, and the score was tied 17-17 at halftime.

The Trojans got the better part of the third quarter and put up two touchdowns. When the fourth quarter started, the Trojans were up 31 to 17. Things didn't look good for UCLA. Not putting any points on the board in the third quarter made Barnes nervous. Not only for the game, but he could see that Donahue had directed the backup quarterback to start warming up. John was determined not to get pulled from the biggest game of his life. He had to make something happen, *now*!

He confidently marched the Bruins down the field and, with a little less than 13 minutes left in the game, Barnes hit JJ Stokes for a 29-yard touchdown making the score 31 to 24, Trojans. Several minutes later, Barnes hit JJ Stokes for a 59 yard gain delivering the ball to the 7 yard line. The Bruin's run game punched it in to tie the score 31-31.

The Trojans punted with a little over four minutes left in the game, and the Bruins took over the ball at their own 4 yard line. Two running plays pushed the ball to the 10 yard line and it was third down and four. By now, Barnes was reading the defense on his own and did not need Coach Neuheisel to flash him signals. He had his own signals with the receivers, and he saw a mismatch. He glanced over at Stokes and gave a gentle nod. What happened next cemented Barnes' fame in UCLA football history.

He had read the defense accurately and knew exactly who he was throwing to. When the ball was snapped, Barnes dropped back seven steps. He tracked his target, JJ Stokes, and drilled a perfect pass straight down the middle. Stokes caught the ball at the 35 and galloped all the way to the end zone for a 90-yard touchdown. Barnes sprinted down the field after Stokes with has arms raised in the air, jumping up and down like a five-year-old who just got a brand new bike. The Bruins were up 38-31 with 3:08 left in the game.

To make things more interesting, the Trojans then marched down the field and scored their own touchdown. The Trojans could have kicked the extra point for a tie. Instead, they went for the two-point conversion and the win. But the pass was knocked down, and the Bruins held the lead at 38-37.

The ensuing onside kick was recovered by the Bruins and John Barnes took the field one last time to run out the clock just like he did in his very first game against San Diego State earlier in the season. As the clock ticked down to zero, John Barnes raised his arms in total victory for the Bruins and for his own personal journey that shocked the football world. As the final seconds ran off the clock, the TV announcer for ESPN stated: "…I'm not sure if you had scripted this script tonight here in Hollywood it would have been done as lavishly as this guy. He has the fourth highest passing game in UCLA history, 385 yards, besides beating his cross-town rival…When you go to a movie theater in 2020, there will probably be a movie about John Barnes."

Coach Terry Donahue put his arm around John that evening and said, "Your life will never be the same." Two years after that game, a sports writer wrote a treatment for a movie script about John Barnes. Ten years after that game, Disney bought the rights to the script. To this day, the script sits on a shelf at Disney Studios.

John Barnes ran off the field that day in 1992 holding the football tightly under his arm. Today that ball sits on a shelf in John's home. Maybe one day that ball will come down off the shelf along with the script at Disney.

***

# Chapter 22
# The Expendables

He played in the NFL for 12 years with the Denver Broncos. He was one of the most ferocious defensive players in franchise history during his career (1983–94). He was voted to play in six Pro Bowls (following the 1985, '86, '87, '89, '91 and '93 seasons); he was named All-AFC and All-NFL four times (1985, ’86, ‘87 and '89); was named AFC Player of the Year by *Football News* in 1986 and played as a Bronco in three Super Bowls: XXI, XXII and XXIV. He finished his career with 1,145 tackles (787 solo) and ranks second in club history with 79.5 sacks. He is in the Denver Broncos Ring of Fame. He also holds the title of “Walk-On.”

Before all the NFL accolades, Karl Mecklenburg was a walk-on and has the stories to go with it. No matter how good Karl was on the field, the title of walk-on granted him a front-row ticket to the painful treatment most walk-ons endure.

It all started in 1978 when Karl was given a one-third scholarship to play football at Augustana College in Sioux Falls, S.D. While the University of Minnesota seemed very high on Mecklenburg, high school signing day came and went leaving Karl with nothing. The Augustana Vikings at least offered a one-third scholarship, the best thing on the table, and Karl took it.

After his second season, it was clear Mecklenburg was a dominating force and his gut was telling him he could play football at a higher level. But he was staying put for the time being. He knew it was a matter of time before his one-third scholarship was turned into a full scholarship as promised by the staff if he played well. When the season ended and Karl was First Team All-World, he was called into the coaches' office. He knew the time had come to say goodbye to two-thirds of the Walk-On life and he would be awarded a full scholarship.

When the coach sat him down, the conversation took a U-turn that blew Mecklenburg away. He was told that since his father was a doctor and could afford the school, they were going to take the one-third scholarship away so they could give it to another player. But of course, Karl was still "their guy" at defensive nose guard! Stunned with that news, Karl departed the school for good, opting to go shopping for a big time program. If he was going to be a walk-on, then he was going to play Division I football. Next stop was the University of Minnesota.

With the 1980 transfer to Minnesota, Mecklenburg would be relegated to the *Beaver Team*, a.k.a. the Scout Team, as he would have to sit out a year and not play in games but he could practice all day long. And that he did and loved it. Yet he was still a walk-on and not high on the priority list as yet.

His leftover issued gear was complete with holey socks, a helmet that didn't fit properly, and a laundry bag with number 114 on it. That was his number as a walk-on, # 114.

Being a walk-on also meant he could not eat at training table unless he performed odd jobs for the athletic department. So he would sweep the floors in the locker room and the weight room from time to time, which would allow him access to training table so he could eat with his teammates. For extra money he got a job as a bouncer at a bar.

At one point during the season, he was having a hard time running and breathing. The trainers told him to tough it out and get back in and practice. He was later diagnosed with walking-pneumonia, but he toughed it out.

He found support in one of his defensive coaches, a young Tony Dungy who 27 years later would go on to coach the Indianapolis Colts to the 2007 Super Bowl Championship. Dungy saw something special in Mecklenburg from the beginning and kept a watchful eye on him. Karl didn't look to start fights in practice to get noticed. He just dominated.

Karl's domination in practice that year proved he was one heck of a football player and worthy of receiving a full scholarship. He got it! And he got a real number too, number 77. As a pre-med major, the scholarship was very helpful as his dream was to become a doctor like his father. Having his education paid for because of football was icing on the cake.

However, this walk-on's journey was not over. During spring practice Mecklenburg blew out his knee and the coaches and trainers feared he would never be the same. In an instant, Karl became expendable. So they asked for their scholarship back! The athletic department cannot take away a scholarship because of an injury, and Karl knew it. He said *no*! With his dreams of being a doctor on the line, and his pre-med education paid for, Karl would not relinquish the scholarship.

Someone on the inside knew if Karl quit, then they would get their scholarship back. Let the hazing begin. The trainers showed little attention to Karl and would stick him in the women's training room during his rehab to humiliate him. This only fueled his fire.

Karl loved two things at this point: school and hitting people on the football field. When practice resumed in the fall, Karl was ready for action and took his anger out on the field. He subsequently led the Gophers in tackles, and it was actually Bo Schembechler of the University of Michigan who nominated Karl for All-Conference.

As a scholarship player and one of the top defensive players in the conference in '81 and '82, he was now getting the respect and accolades he deserved. He did not forget who he was or where he came from, however. He looked after his fellow walk-on teammates. He would often ask how each walk-on was doing. If a guy was discouraged, Mecklenburg would give him words of encouragement. Many a walk-on wanted to quit, throw in the towel. But Karl motivated them to stay the course and fight through the adversity. He did it because he truly cared for them. He was one of them, and he said being a walk-on is a brotherhood.

Mecklenburg states his walk-on years at Augustana and first year at Minnesota were the years he grew up. Those were the building blocks for his lessons in life. Those were the years he started to understand that success would only be realized with overcoming major obstacles and if you don't have obstacles, then you're not pushing hard enough.

His advice for high school seniors who are thinking of walking-on is to first pick a school that has what you want to study. Remembering that only a very small percentage of players make it in the NFL (less than 3 percent) and those who do make it last only three and a half years on average. So your school work has to be your number-one focus. Next, pick a school where you will be comfortable. If you're a city kid, don't pick Nebraska or a school in a very rural area. If you're a born and bred warm weather fanatic, don't pick a school that has near freezing temperatures.

In fact, Karl recently wrote a whole book with advice for high school athletes, coaches, and parents titled *Heart of a Student Athlete: All-Pro Advice for Competitors and Their Families*.

Karl Mecklenburg rose from being an expendable college walk-on to a twelfth-round NFL draft pick to a pro career that included six Pro Bowls and three Super Bowl appearances. He went from being expendable to being inspirational!

***

# Chapter 23
# I'm No Mannequin

All too often, assistant coaches are so focused on the development of their recruited scholarship players that they conveniently forget about the walk-on players, and use them as bait, fodder, and tackling dummies; a.k.a. human mannequins.

They see the walk-ons as part of the equipment used to develop their star players, the guys they recruited, the guys they invested money in, and most importantly, the guys they expect to play on Saturdays. They want their boys to be "All-Everything." This makes them appear as a good coach while padding their own résumés.

Individual drills in practice are centered on improving the scholarship player. Walk-ons are used to push those players to the next level, to drive them to play better and hit harder. Those walk-ons soon discover what it is like to be a human piñata.

Walk-ons, including myself, and other Game Day Capable Walk-Ons, take great offense to being defenseless. Some drills are initiated in order to teach tackling runners from behind, or stripping the ball from a runner after they pass the line of scrimmage. It is in those drills where the human mannequins are blind-sided from behind in a violent blow forcing them on a collision course with the ground. You are extremely vulnerable and yet the coaches are screaming for you to properly participate in the drill which really means; blindly jog down the field and expose yourself in a susceptible manner, put yourself in grave danger risking great injury so my scholarship player can hit you from behind at full speed and take you to the ground with a powerful and ferocious thud. Oh, awesome, sign me up!

With the wind knocked out of you, gasping for air, you are then expected to get up after that crushing blow and body slam to the ground, get back in line and do it again for the next scholarship player who is salivating with his own quest to be the best.

There was an "exercise" called the Fumble Drill. A player would carry the ball somewhat loosely and head down the field on a slow jog. A second player would race after the first coming up from behind him at full speed. In an instant he would incorporate a punch at the ball or a mighty slap with an arm-over or arm-under technique with one hand and throw a body wrap around with the other. At the very same time their goal was to catapult their body through the ball carrier taking him to the ground.

Would you like to guess on where the walk-on was in this process? A) The one holding the ball and jogging blindly down the field or B) The player running full blast from behind and decking the ball carrier while slapping at the ball? Anyone? Anyone?

Do you see the problem? Well, for starters when you jog blindly down the field and get attacked from behind, the chances of injury to the ball carrier is increased tenfold. Twisted ankles, Achilles tendon tears and pulls are the norm as they come crashing down on the back of your legs. A score of other injuries could and would occur as the "tackler" with all the momentum and advantages would be bearing down on the hapless "ball carrier" from behind. Talk about setting someone up to fail and get hurt. Wow!

I had my own dreams of proving myself and playing on Saturdays. If I were injured I sure as heck would never get that chance. I was not about to throw my entire college career away by engaging in a drill set to crush my body and my dreams. These drills were markedly different than the head-to-head drills, which I cherished, where both players had an equal chance to win. I decided that was NOT going to happen to me. So, I devised a plan.

I would hold the ball a few inches away from my body, so loosely it would fall out if the wind blew. Then as I heard the "tackler" bear down on me from behind, I would basically release the ball and jump to my left as I was just about to feel his hot breath on the back of my neck. The ball would drop and the tackler would fall forward without landing on the back of my legs.

Well, the kickers and punters had a fantastic laugh over this but the coaches went ballistic!! "Damn you, Lavin! How the hell are we supposed to practice the fumble drill when you drop the ball and jump out of the way???" The coach was so upset with me. I looked him in the eye and said; "Coach, I don't like to practice bad habits. If you really want me in this drill, let me run full speed and hold the ball just like they do in a game."

Well, that totally rational and logical suggestion did not go over too well with Coach Tom Roggeman. After he cursed me out, he told me to get the hell away from him. So, I went to the break area and enjoyed some refreshing water with the kickers while I watched several other walk-ons go through this drill and get pummeled.

Now, let me totally explain myself here so no one thinks I am a smart-aleck who obnoxiously confronts coaches. I don't believe in that. I believe you show coaches respect from start to finish. I was not trying to be disrespectful. I was actually trying to tell the coach in so many words that I planned on being a player on this team on Saturdays and running with the ball. I don't want to practice fumbling because that is exactly what running backs practice NOT to do in their individual drills. I don't want a 250 lb. linebacker coming down on the back of my legs and risking serious injury. If I get injured, I will for sure NOT achieve my dream and additionally, I don't want to walk with a limp the rest of my life because of a ridiculous fumble drill that broke my leg in three places. I spent all my time not only trying to prove the coaches wrong, but prove myself right. I had to prove that I could play at this level and that I did deserve a scholarship, and I did deserve to play on Saturdays. Participating in this "death drill" was just something I felt was not right.

If any coach thinks I am wrong in any way, shape, or forum, I would encourage them to suit up and be the "ball carrier." I would also simply say to them, "You consider yourself to be a great coach right? Well, come up with a drill that your scholarship guys can practice where you don't risk killing the walk-ons you don't care about!"

I loved Coach Roggeman. Always did and always will. I know he respected me because I went toe–to-toe with his best players daily in the drills and live scrimmages. Because of this, I told him my feelings about the "Fumble Drill." Deep down I truly believe he knew I was right and I should not be engaging in that drill. I fought his best guys day in and day out and he could always count on me to stand up and test his linebackers. Our one-on-one drills were ugly, brutal, and extremely violent. There were many drills where I had to line up at fullback 4 yards deep and sprint full blast at his linebacker, also 4 yards deep, coming at me full speed. The 8 yard distance between us closed in the blink of an eye as we attacked each other with all our might. The helmet smacking could be heard from blocks away. It was loud and powerful.

Walk-ons are free players. Coaches depend on walk-ons to help their scholarship players reach their potential. They need walk-ons in practice. So, don't set up walk-ons for injury! Don't set us up for failure! Teach your scholarship guys to be better. No running back in a game is going to bust through the line and then start jogging. Step up to the plate and teach your scholarship guys to go after the hard running walk-on ball carrier holding the ball tightly – like they do in a real game.

I know that football is a violent game. The risk of injury is common and the danger of life-changing damage is prevalent. Why do we want to chance increasing these odds with very bad fumble drills? But, perhaps that is just my Achilles tendon talking.

***

# Chapter 24
# Punt Team U-turn

I was a freshman walk-on in the fall of 1988 for the Trojans, and of course spent the year on scout team and never saw a down of game playing time, so I "redshirted" during my "true freshman" year. However, I created havoc on scout team and fighting was an everyday occurrence in practice. That earned me respect both from my teammates and apparently the coaching staff.

In my second year on campus—my redshirt freshman year as an athlete and my sophomore year academically—I was placed as a backup on special teams. I was listed on the depth chart as second-string on both the kickoff and punt return teams. To be a walk-on redshirt freshman listed as the number 2 backup was virtually unheard of, and I was pretty proud I had climbed the ladder so early on. But that was just not good enough for me. I wanted to play, and I was still the number 5 fullback behind four scholarship players.

In the second contest of the year, I played in the LA Coliseum during the Utah State game in the fourth quarter while we were winning 66 to 10. I was thrown in at fullback for about six or seven plays, and I actually was given the ball twice. The first carry was for 6 yards and a first down. A few plays later, I got the nod again on a third and one and I broke through the line, spun off the linebacker in a 360-degree move and was pulled down after gaining 14 yards and another first down. Two carries for 20 yards and a 10-yard per carry average was shown in the paper the next day. Hellooooo Nelly! I was making my move!

While it was incredible to set foot on the Coliseum floor in that game, technically it was still meaningless mop-up time. I was ecstatic to get in, but the rest of the team was already celebrating on the sidelines, and the fans were all leaving.

My next opportunity to play in a game came later that season in late 1989, our last regular season game against UCLA. That was a week that was both tragic and exhilarating.

This was going to be different than the Utah State game. It was against UCLA, our cross-town rival and I was going to be starting on the punt return special team! At no point in the season did I travel with the team, yet I was still listed as the number 2 man on kickoff, punt return, and punt block. I was positioned on the left side of the line on punt return and punt block as we had 10 guys lined up on the line of scrimmage and my spot was located just outside the right offensive tackle. I had blocked so many punts in practice that our special teams coach, Bobby April, put me in as backup to Kurt Barber, our starting outside linebacker. Barber would later be selected with the forty second pick in the second round of the 1992 NFL Draft by the New York Jets.

News came a week before the '89 UCLA game that Kurt's father had passed away. It was sad to see him so down, and he took the next plane home to Kentucky that Monday to be with his family. It was a terrible time for Kurt as anyone can imagine. On that Monday, at practice, with Kurt on the flight heading home, I was tapped to be Barber's replacement the next Saturday for the home game at the LA Coliseum against the Bruins.

Out of a tragedy that happened to my teammate, it was my opportunity to shine. This was my time to get in a real game, to start on a special team, to play in front of 90,000 people including my parents. In addition, the game was to be televised on ABC. Wow! Everyone I know will be able to see me play. I was ecstatic and walking on air all week.

Monday through Thursday I was out there on the field, starting on punt return and punt block. I blocked a couple of punts in practice during the week and my boys in the cheering section, the kickers, were yelling for me. Even a few coaches threw in, "Good job, Lavin" a few times during the week. Those comments made me feel like I was really making progress. I was at my highest emotional state since I had first stepped foot on campus at USC in August 1988.

The travel squad list was posted on the bulletin board outside the locker room after practice every Thursday. The Traveling 60 we called it. Only 60 players could travel. Even for home games, only 60 players could stay at the team hotel in Los Angeles. All 100 plus players got to dress and be on the sidelines during the game, but 40 players had to find their own way to the stadium. This was going to be my first travel. I might sound like a giddy grade-school kid, but this was a huge deal for me. It is something you work towards. If your name is on the Traveling 60, you are most likely playing. It was an incredible feeling for this 19-year-old Redshirt Freshman Walk-on!

All week long I kept my parents posted. I spoke to them every night that week, supplying updates. They were thrilled and so happy for me. They kept my brothers posted and word was spreading to all our friends and relatives. Since the game was going to be on ABC, I think just about every person we knew as a family was either going to the game or would be watching on TV.

After practice on Thursday, I was excited to get off the field and head to the locker room. I could not wait to see my name on the Travel Squad list for the first time ever. As my teammates and I walked down the hallway, I had a bit of urgency in my step and walked faster than the others. When I got to the board, I looked up with pride. I looked from top to bottom, bottom to top. My name was not on the list. It was in alphabetical order and it took one second to see my name was not there. Yet I continued looking hoping they put my name at the bottom, or perhaps they

# LAVIN

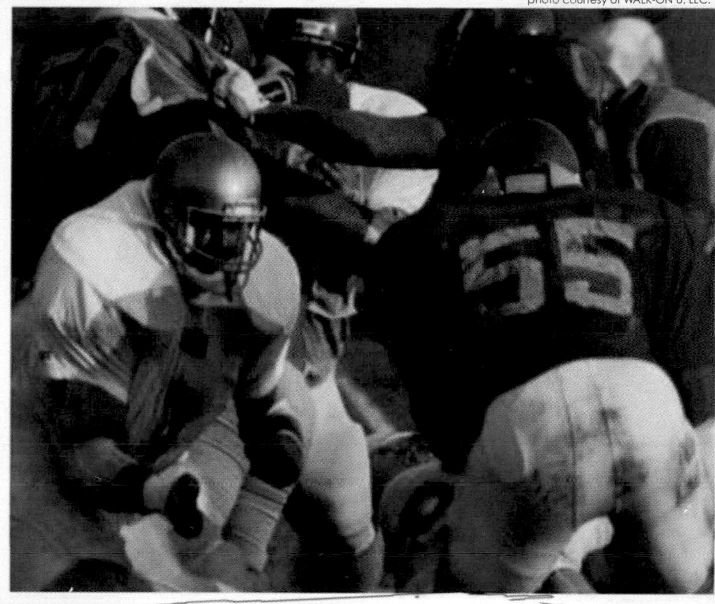

photo courtesy of WALK-ON U, LLC.

**TIM LAVIN** wearing "Golden Dome" helmet during ND practice week to make a walk-on statement.

**IM LAVIN**
**uthor/Founder**
Valk-On: University of Southern California

photo courtesy of BILL EMERSON

**BILL EMERSON, *Quicken Loans***
**Chief Executive Officer**
Walk-On: Penn State University

photo courtesy of THE ASSOCIATED PRESS

**KEVIN A. PLANK, UNDER ARMOUR®**
**Chief Executive Officer &Chairman of the Board**
Walk-On: University of Maryland

photo courtesy of THE ASSOCIATED PRESS

photo courtesy of THE ASSOCIATED PRESS

**CLAY MATTHEWS**
NFL First Round Draft Pick, 4 Pro-Bowls, 2x All Pro
NFC Defensive Player of the Year
Super Bowl Champion
Walk-On: University of Southern California

**J.J. WATT**
NFL First Round Draft Pick, 11th Overall
AFC Defensive Player of the Year 2012
Walk-On: Wisconsin

photo courtesy of THE ASSOCIATED PRESS

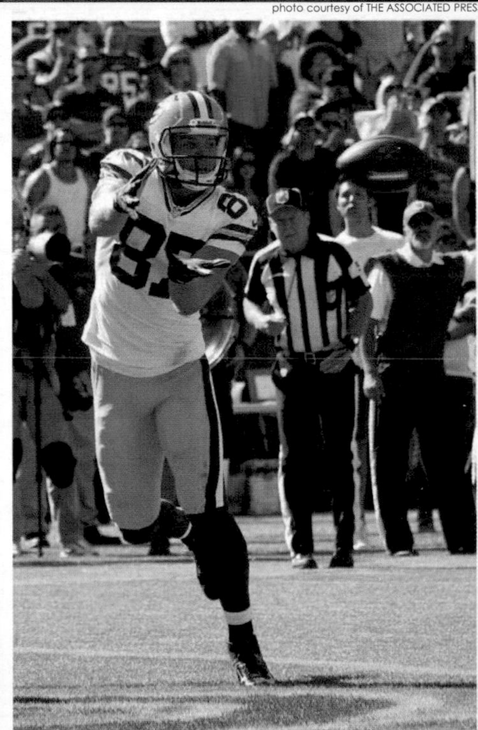
photo courtesy of THE ASSOCIATED PRESS

**LOU HOLTZ**
Head Coach, College Football
for over 40+ Years
National Champion 1988
Walk-On: Kent State

**JORDY NELSON**
Super Bowl Champion
NFL 2nd Round Draft Pick
Walk-On: Kansas State

photo courtesy of THE ASSOCIATED PRESS

**TOM OSBORNE**
Head Coach for over 3 Decades at Nebraska
3 National Championships
*Architect of Husker Walk On Program*

photo courtesy of THE ASSOCIATED PRESS

**TERRY DONAHUE**
Head Coach UCLA, 1976-1995
2x Pac-10 Coach of the Year
Walk-On: UCLA

photo courtesy of THE ASSOCIATED PRESS

**DABO SWINNEY**
Head Coach Clemson
2011 ACC Champions
Walk-On: Alabama

photo courtesy of THE ASSOCIATED PRESS

**KEVIN SUMLIN**
Head Coach Texas A&M
3x Conference Coach of the Year
Walk-On: Purdue University

photo courtesy of THE ASSOCIATED PRESS

photo courtesy of THE ASSOCIATED

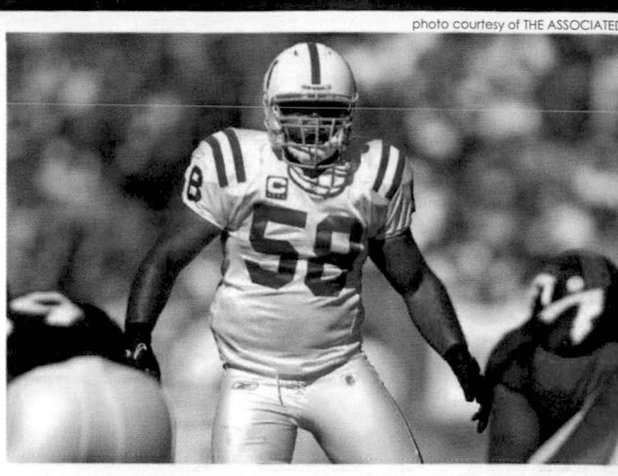

**GARRY BRACKETT**
9 Year NFL Veteran, 2 Year AFC Champion
Super Bowl XLI Champion
Walk-On: Rutgers

**MIKE SHERRARD**
11 Year NFL Veteran
1st Round NFL Draft Pick
18th Overall
Walk-On: University of California Los Angeles

photo courtesy of THE ASSOCIATED PRESS

photo courtesy of THE ASSOCIATED PRESS

**OREN O'NEAL**
With one Strong Heart and only one good Lung he was a 6th Round Draft Pick
Walk-On: Arkansas State

**KARL MECKLENBURG**
12 Year NFL Veteran, 6 Pro Bowls,
4x All-NFL and AFC, 3 Super Bowls
Walk-On: University of Minnesota

sandwiched me further up or down the list by mistake. But it just wasn't there. I went through all 60 names and there was no Lavin.

Feeling like my heart had been ripped out of my chest, I made my way upstairs to the coach's office to see what went wrong. I didn't stop at the assistant's desk to ask permission to go toward the back where all the offices were tucked away. I was still in full dress with helmet in hand and went straight to the back room. Some coaches were gathering to discuss the day's practice when I approached them. "What's up Lav?" I walked over and grabbed Special-Teams Coach April by the arm and pulled him aside, away from the other coaches.

"Lav, what's up?" he asked. Struggling to get my words out, I spoke in a slight whisper. Partly because I didn't want to make a scene in front of the other coaches and partly because I was so filled with anger and emotion it was hard to get the words out. "My name is not on the list."

"What?" he said bending near me to stick his ear closer to my mouth.

"My name is not on the Travel Squad list" I responded.

Putting his hand on my shoulder, he said with a smile, "Lav, we could not put you on the travel squad list just because you are starting on special teams tomorrow. We could not drop someone off the list; they need to be there too. And Barber is flying back tomorrow night so he will be in the team hotel."

Still unsure I said, "I'm still starting on punt return Saturday?"

"Hell yes, Lavin, you're my guy! Barber will play on defense like always, but you are on punt return!"

The weight on my shoulders lifted, and my heart rose back into my chest. Thank God!

OK, so I'm not staying in the hotel tomorrow night with the team. That blows. *But* I will be starting on punt return/punt block and that's what really counts. I remember having mixed feelings again. Part of me felt like I was a Trojan football player. Part of me felt like I was not even on the team. Do my Traveling 60 teammates even know I am supposed to start Saturday? Do they even know my name was not on the travel list? I felt so high and so low at the same time. It was almost indescribable.

Friday's practice came, and it was just a walk-through. We were in our sweats and helmets—no other pads. We were on the field for less than an hour, and the offense and defense ran a handful of plays. The last 15 minutes we covered all special teams. Coach yelled out "Kickoff," and 11 guys hit the field at their respective positions. Then, in case of injury to a player, we needed to know who was on second team in those spots. So the coach would yell, "Crane out."

Pretending that Bob Crane got hurt, his replacement, the second-team guy, would sprint to that position. We would go through all 11 guys on each special team. I waited nervously as we went through every spot on the kick-off team, then the hands team (for onside kicks), then kickoff return, then the punt team. After hearing 44 names getting called off the field, I finally heard what I had been waiting for: "Punt Return Team!"

I sprinted to my spot on the line of scrimmage. The coaches looked over each spot and yelled, "OK, good!" I breathed a sigh of relief; now I was *sure* I was starting.

After that Friday practice, the Traveling 60 hit the showers then jumped on the team bus heading to the Hyatt Hotel in downtown LA. I showered and walked back to my apartment by myself. It was so odd and uncomfortable to know that I was going to be playing the next day, yet I was not allowed to be with my teammates. I would not be there for the team bus ride to the hotel. I would not be there for the team's evening meal, the team movie, or the team meeting. I was going to be home by myself. It was Friday night and my roommates, who were not football players, were out and about doing their thing. I was restless. I paced around my apartment looking for something to do. I wondered what my teammates were doing right at that moment. They were all together, as a team. I was a team member, but by myself, on the other side of town. It was way too early to go to sleep. The flip-flopping of emotions dwelled within me yet again. It was the longest night.

I was to report at 10 a.m. to the LA Coliseum locker room. That's when the team buses were to arrive. When I landed by foot at the fence leading down the famous Coliseum tunnel, the security checked my name on the team roster and I made my way down the tunnel. The team buses had not arrived yet so I walked into a completely empty locker room. I looked around and found my jersey hanging in the cramped 8 foot by 8 foot four-man cubicle locker. The Traveling 60 and other scholarship guys (even those who did not travel) had the traditional big lockers that you can sit inside along the giant walls encompassing the wide open area of the locker room. Adjacent to this area and along the back walls were encapsulated cubicles that the walk-ons called home.

Four guys had to get fully dressed with all our pads in these cramped quarters. Again, I felt more like a nuisance than a team member. To be fair, it was an issue of available room and not one of punishment. Nevertheless, it was still a horrible feeling to be sure. I didn't feel like a starter that day, but I was determined to prove my worthiness. I committed to make an impact that would be long-lasting. I couldn't wait to hit the field!

We did our normal warm-up routine and I looked for, and found my mom and dad up in their usual parents' section seats. I could always find my mother with her big blond hair. That is what I zeroed in on while stretching before the game. Once I found them I could relax. I knew they arrived safely and I was just so happy to play in front of them that day. It was a thrilling moment and I was ready for this game to start.

Shortly after 12:30 p.m. the game kicked off with 90,000 fans in frenzy. I never rooted so hard for our defense before. Three and out, three and out, was what I was wishing for. I don't remember how many plays it took, but it was not three. UCLA got a couple first downs but then we held them and it was fourth down. My moment had finally come. The helmet was on, chin strap was snapped, and my heart was pounding!

It is the job of one of our GA coaches to quickly yell out the 11 names of the guys about to hit the field. As third down approached Coach Jeff Brown started yelling out; "Punt return right here, punt return right here!" A small crowd of players gathered as several of the other punt block team players were on defense and already out on the field. Coach Brown continued yelling out the 11 individual names. Third down was happening at that very moment. Names are being read aloud. The ball is in the air. I am counting the names he screams out. That's 6 names, there's 7, 8, 9...I am not hearing my name, but I know it is coming and, and, and, and… "Incomplete pass and fourth down." We hit the field on a full sprint, and on my second and third step onto the field I hear the tenth name and then the eleventh: BARBER!

I slammed on the breaks three or four yards onto the field, and screamed back at Coach; "NO, NOT BARBER! LAVIN!!!"

Coach Brown was waving me back to the sideline as the punt return guys were running to mid-field.

"Lavin, come back, come back." I screamed back, "Coach, I've been on punt return all week!" Still hesitant to come off the field, I was frozen. "No, no, Lavin, come back. They made the change. They made the change, last night, at the hotel."

I took three steps back to the sidelines and looked at Coach Brown with eyes the size of silver dollars. "What!" I demanded to know immediately.

I could tell he felt horrible when he looked at me so sincerely and said, "You mean, nobody told you?" I could see that while he looked into my eyes his own heart was dropping. "Lav, Lav, they made the change last night. Last night in the special teams meeting at the hotel, they made the change for Barber to go back on punt return."

Without uttering another word, I walked away from the coach and found a spot on the bench and sat down. I looked across the field up into the stands and I could see my folks looking down at me. My father was peering down at me holding binoculars. I was humiliated. Aside from the football aspect of being totally devastated, the human element was what took its toll on me. My parents had longed for this day. They were so proud of this moment because they knew what it meant to me. My brothers, all of our friends, our relatives; they all were watching on television waiting for that very moment. I never made it on the field that day.

Coach April was in the press box and had made it to the locker room at halftime before the players got there. As we came running in, the coach was standing right there to greet the players as we entered. When I saw him, I tried to shoot him the dirtiest look from hell that I could as we made eye contact. I think he immediately knew what happened and quickly looked away as other players were coming in behind me. I don't think I spoke a word to anyone the rest of the game or afterwards. I just showered and walked home dejected, embarrassed, and humiliated.

On Monday morning, I walked into Coach April's office and just sat in front of him without saying a word. I just stared at him. He looked back at me and just crumbled. "Lav, I am so sorry. I am so, so sorry. You were supposed to have been told and we, as coaches, dropped the ball. I am so sorry."

I asked why he did it. He stated that while they were in special teams meetings Friday night, Barber made his way back to the team hotel. He felt bad for Barber and didn't think it was right for him to lose his starting position just because his father died. I jumped back at him with a stern voice and pounded my fist on his desk, "He started on Defense! He still got to play! This was my only hope of playing. This was my time, my job, my opportunity! Everyone I know was watching for my big shot. I got nothing!"

Coach April just shook his head back and forth knowing they screwed up big time and that they let me down by not letting me play, and they let me down by dropping the ball in not telling me I had been replaced. He just kept saying "Lav, I know, I know. I am so sorry." Without saying another word I just stood up and walked out of his office.

***

# Chapter 25
# The Growing Frustration

As I entered my redshirt sophomore season (year three), I felt my time was due. I had a very successful spring and fall training camp. I was promised a full-ride because of my work in spring camp yet had received only a half-scholarship. I knew at the very least I was going to be on special teams and be in the top three for the fullback slot.

We opened the first game of the season against Syracuse at Giants Stadium in the Meadowlands in the College Football Kickoff Classic. I traveled but never made it onto the field. The next two games against Penn State and Washington were the same, as I saw no action at all. Frustration and anger was building. I would have a great practice and wouldn't hear a word from the special teams coach or my running-back coach about moving up the ladder. One day I made my way to my apartment after a grueling but very successful practice. Unfortunately, it had appeared to go unrecognized yet again. I was furious. It was the week of our fourth game against Ohio State at the Horseshoe in Columbus, Ohio.

I had been through a month of training camp plus three games into the season. I was still stuck on the scout team. But I was really making things happen, opening up holes for our scout team tailback, getting great kick out blocks and constantly fighting with defensive players. We were making yards, getting first downs and pushing around a defense that was ranked in the top 10 in the nation. Scout team was made up of walk-ons and young scholarship guys waiting for their big chance to move up the ladder.

It was a foregone conclusion the younger scholarship players got the nod to move up the ranks any time the coaches got frustrated with an upperclassman not doing a great job or if an injury occurred. In other words, I was not witnessing the old-fashion philosophy "Work hard and you will rise up the ranks." From my perspective the younger scholarship players were just standing in line, waiting for their name to be called, and they knew it would be sooner or later.

But for me, I felt like no matter how hard I worked, no matter how much I dominated in practice, my name was not going to be called to run plays with the first and second string offense. The feeling was like trying to walk up an escalator that is coming down. That was my frustration.

We had just finished another full-padded live practice on the Tuesday before Ohio State. I felt I had another great practice. I engaged my blocks and opened up holes for the tailback to get through. Not one player got past me when I set up to block on pass plays, and I completely frustrated those I blocked on the run plays. I just felt like I could not fail as I seemed to be successful down after down, snap after snap, so much so that the defensive players wanted to fight me virtually after every play. The defensive coaches were screaming at their specific position player's non-stop and I constantly was finding myself the source of their frustration. *Damn it! Run it again! And don't let Lavin kick you out!*

I don't know why, but I guess I was just looking for some confirmation that my play was appreciated. Here I was, just a little ol' walk-on, now with a half-scholarship, practicing in a live scrimmage against one of the top defenses in the country, and I was making things happen. I'm not saying I won every single battle, but I was playing like a guy that needed to be on the field on Saturday; I know that.

Our Graduate Assistant (GA) Coach, Ken Zampese (Coach Z we called him), was in my corner. He was in charge of running the scout team offense. I did get tons of encouragement from Coach Z. Every time I won the battle on a play and the defensive coaches got all upset I would run back to the huddle and Coach Z would be smiling at me. "Way to go Lav! Way to go!!" I loved his support. I needed it. In fact, he was the only person within the whole program at that point in time that made me feel like I mattered. I remember going to him often just to talk before we went out to the practice field.

I liked my teammates very much. But, technically the fullbacks were my competitors and socializing with them before practice didn't sit well with me. They were in front of me on the depth chart and there was nothing enjoyable about that. My other walk-on buddies, my cronies on the kicking squad, Marc Preston and Grant Runnerstrum, were off doing kicking drills or playing hacky-sack so there were not really too many people I felt a real connection to other than Coach Z. He was my confidant. He was my connection to the staff, my internal link to finding out if I was going to get an opportunity to play on special teams on Saturday. To this day he probably has no idea that the bond I had with him meant everything to me. But Coach Z was a GA and he did not have the power or authority to put me on special teams or move me up the depth-chart ladder at fullback. All he could do was talk me up in the coaches meetings and let them take the ball and run with it.

After that great Tuesday practice when I was ignored by the staff again, I felt like I was going to explode. Does anyone recognize what I am doing? Does anyone care? I went home after practice with my blood boiling.

Pacing through my bedroom I had the urge to hit something to unleash some fury. In a fit of unbridled frustration I pictured myself punching my bedroom wall. I cocked back my fist ready to put a hole through the drywall. In the blink of an eye I pictured my fist connecting with the wall and I immediately thought to myself; "what if there is a 2" x 4" wood stud right on the other side of this drywall?" I stopped my fist inches before connecting. Instead, I looked down at my bed and beat the crap out of my pillow.

After I cooled down and was thankful I hadn't hit the wall. I called Jim Walsh. I remember saying to him; "Jim, why are they doing this to me?" He always knew what to say to make me feel better. His words sent shivers down my spine. "Tim, believe me! They *are* talking about you right now. In their coaches meeting right at this very second, they are watching film of today's practice and they are saying to each other, 'Lavin is not your typical walk-on.' They may not be saying anything to you now, but your time is coming."

He also told me that I had the great fortune and opportunity of going up against some of the best players in the country which was going to make me a far better football player than the fullbacks at the other end of the field who were practicing against scout team players.

As much as I wanted to stay mad, I almost couldn't. I felt like I was winning, even if the coaches were not talking to me, other than Coach Z. Jim made me feel that behind closed doors my name was being thrown around like a hot potato in the coaches' office.

My attitude was steadfast and focused. I wasn't going to let them build themselves up by trying to keep me down. I thought to myself; "They may not want walk-ons to play on Saturday, but they won't tear me apart and they will not beat me or break me, physically or emotionally."

Before practice the next day, Coach Zampese walked by me and winked. "Keep it up Lav, they're talking about you." I grabbed his arm to keep him from walking past me. "*What!* What are they saying?"

He just smiled at me and said; "They love everything about you. So, just keep it up!" And away he walked. A shot of adrenaline went through my veins. Jim Walsh was right! Behind closed doors, they were talking about me.

That Wednesday afternoon practice turned out to be something special. We ran through all of our drills and scrimmages and then it was time for Special Teams. I ran over to Coach Z to get ready for the scout Punt Block Team like I always did. He looked at me and smiled. "Make this your day, Lav!"

***

# Chapter 26
# My Time Has Come

The anger still seethed within me and I had resigned myself to thinking, well if they won't play me on Saturday then I will just have to make one hell of a statement in practice. After being inspired by Coach Zampese's encouragement I lined up for the Punt Block Scout Team.

The Punt Block Team was the special team, on which when we played UCLA the previous season, I got replaced. I had more than a little extra fire in my belly for this scout team because of that embarrassment and I was ready to explode. The whole team observed special teams and everyone was at the end of the field watching together. The punt team would be kicking from the 10 yard line. Twenty-two players lined up on the field and another 80 players surround us on both sidelines and throughout the end zone. Every assistant coach stood nearby to bear witness as well. With over 125 pairs of eyeballs zeroed in on this play I was ready to make my statement. The gloves were off. Let's roll.

This would be my most defining moment of practice and perhaps my career. We lined up and the ball was snapped. I was located in the gap between the long snapper and the left guard. The punter (Marc Preston) was right-footed. When the ball was snapped I shot through the gap faster than the blink of an eye and sprinted up field. The ball was kicked right into my hands! BLOCKED!

Statement! With adrenaline shooting through my entire body I may have inadvertently acted a tad antagonistic, and I don't recommend you try this at home. As the ball bounced backwards into the end zone I went crazy! I jumped up and down yelling like a mad man and went sprinting over to Coach April. Pointing my finger right at him from just a few feet away, I screamed; "PUT ME ON YOUR PUNT BLOCK TEAM! PUT ME ON YOUR PUNT BLOCK TEAM!!"

The entire team was watching and yelling for me. "WAY TO GO LAVIN! T-LAV IN THE HOUSE!!! HE'S GOT YOUR NUMBER PUNT TEAM!" And then I heard one voice scream out, "HE'S A WALK-ON, BABY!" followed by laughter and cheers. The roar of my teammates fired me up even more.

I am not sure if Coach April was more upset that the punt got blocked or that I got in his face pleading, albeit in an antagonistic way, to be a starter while the team was cheering me on. April screamed at me to "shut the F%$# Up" and get back to the huddle.

The coaches yelled at our left guard to step a little bit closer to the foot of the long snapper so he could stop me from coming in. We lined up for the second punt and the ball was snapped. All was quiet, like in slow motion, with 100 plus guys watching this very play. I was coming full steam ahead and broke through the gap, again! I jumped as high as I could and immediately two slaps were heard. Boom, boom!

The first slap was that of the ball being kicked by the punter. The second slap was that of the ball hitting my hands. I blocked it again!! Bam! Statement!

Yes, I went crazy a second time and the team was jumping up and down with several guys racing over to me from the sidelines to jump on me. It was an AWESOME feeling. And yes, I gambled again and went racing over to Coach Bobby April who had already started his rant on the left guard.

"PUT ME ON YOUR PUNT BLOCK TEAM, PUT ME ON YOUR PUNT BLOCK TEAM. THEY CAN'T STOP ME, THEY CAN'T STOP ME!" April again screamed at me to "shut the F&%$ Up" and get back to the huddle. I knew I was pushing his buttons and not sure how this gamble would pay off but I felt I had absolutely nothing to lose. Teammates continued to mob me on the field, slapping my shoulder pads and helmet. The other assistant coaches screamed for the players to get off the field so we could run the play again. At the same time they all were trying to hide their smiles. The coaches were enjoying this too.

We huddled up and Coach Zampese came in the huddle. He looked at me with the biggest smile on his face. "Way to go Lav, great job!" That was all the encouragement I needed.

Coach Smith came running over and actually moved Brian Tuliau, the up-back and personal protector, located a few feets behind the right guard, over to the left side behind the left guard – right in front of me. I would now have to break through the left guard, but then power past or go through the up-back, Tuliau, to get to the punter.

The up-back is supposed to be lined up on the same side as the punters kicking leg. But, after I blocked two punts in a row, I was creating havoc for the coaches and they were realigning a guy just to take care of me. This was gorgeous and I loved every minute of it.

We now lined up for the third punt. I knew Brian still had the responsibility of the right side, the kicking leg side. I also knew that just by his presence he would create a problem for me. I was hoping that he was thinking… if the left guard could get just one good punch to my right shoulder pad and if he could get a one-hand punch on my left side then that would slow me down enough to get the punt off.

A new course was set in my mind. I moved slightly closer to the long snapper and would shoot past him and the left guard but go slightly right of Tuliau, making him think I was going off-course. I knew he would get a hand check and try to shove me away while looking back to the right side; the kicking leg side, and most importantly his responsibility side.

With that in mind I got as low as I could to blow past the guard, turned my body sideways and used an arm-over-swim technique over Tuliau's left shoulder pad and broke free. I then jumped as high as I could and somehow, in some strange way, I managed to get my hand on the ball for the third blocked punt in a row!

Pandemonium erupted! Over 80 players poured onto the field in a full sprint at me and I was dog-piled and buried on the turf. I heard screaming and cheering above me that was deafening. But, I was also at the bottom of the biggest dog pile in history. At that moment I started to lose my breath and the players at the bottom of the pile saw my face changing color. They started screaming for everyone to get off of us and within mere seconds twenty plus players were screaming; "Get him up, get him up, get him up! Everyone get off us! Get off! Get up! Get up!!" Thankfully, I was brought to my feet pretty quickly and caught my breath. The players still had me surrounded and in their sheer excitement for me they were pushing and shoving me all over the place.

I was beyond excited and felt I had more than made my statement. Again, I looked at Coach April. He was staring at me in disbelief and shaking his head as he walked up to his punt team players who failed to stop me for the third time in a row. This time I toned it down a bit and instead of pointing at him; I pointed to myself and said "START ME! START ME!"

I could hear Coach April going nuts. I remember him screaming; "THIS DID NOT JUST HAPPEN!!! DAMN IT! ARE YOU KIDDING ME? HOW THE HELL IS HE GETTING THROUGH YOU GUYS?"

He then moved the guard over foot to foot with the long snapper and moved Brian right in the gap splitting the two linemen, just inches behind them. On the next punt attempt both players focused on me and only me. I did not get in the backfield that time, but they had to realign two players to stop me. The statement I wanted to make had been made.

When practice ended I got pats on my back from the field all the way into the locker room. It was a fantastic feeling. Regardless of what the coaches were going to do with me, I knew that my fellow teammates recognized and respected me. That meant the world to me and I took great pride in myself, and what I had just accomplished.

The next day was Thursday and I reported to Coach Z for my daily pre-practice briefing. For the rest of my life, I'll remember this conversation more vividly than any other talk we ever had. "Lav, I love having you with me. The bad news is you're not with me anymore. They want you to run with the 1's and 2's today."

I was very happy they wanted me to run with the starters, but I did not allow myself to get too excited. I knew the walk-on world all too well. I was cautiously optimistic. We'll see where they really place me on the depth chart and if they take me to the Ohio State game.

That day we ran through special teams. Coach April had me on all five of them. I was on the Punt Team, the Punt Return / Punt Block Team, Kickoff and Kickoff Return Teams and also the Hands Team.

Punt Team was typically all defensive players because they tackle for a living so I was pretty happy I was being looked at even though I was an offensive fullback. I could catch the ball pretty well, but the Hands Team was always a bunch of wide receivers with really good hands to catch the onside kick. But there I was on the front line with a bunch of receivers. Very interesting so far but again, I was not going to get my hopes up just yet. I was excited they were looking at me. But, I had been down this road before and there's a lot of shuffling during practice. Guys get their hopes up and then Thursday or Friday new things happen and names get moved around.

Thursday is the day they post the travel squad list on the bulletin board outside of our locker room. Coach April had me lined up in practice as the starter, but never actually said, "You're starting." So, I was still in limbo. The team flies to Ohio State tomorrow. Am I going or are they setting me up to start the following week? I just had no idea of their motive or intentions.

After practice we walked to the locker room as always. The anxiety raced through my stomach like it had so many times before. I approached the board and looked up. About half way down the list I saw LAVIN!

I was traveling. I had made the list! I was going to Columbus, Ohio to play in the Horseshoe against the Buckeyes. My time had come and I could not wait to get home to call my parents and my brothers. From that day forward Coach April started me on all of his special teams for the rest of the year. Needless to say, I made him proud.

Incidentally, during the Ohio State game, a 35 – 26 Trojan win truncated by a lightning storm, the punt block was executed perfectly. I broke through the line and the up-back (the personal protector) had to shift over to block me. This freed up my teammate who actually blocked the punt while another picked up the bouncing ball and raced it back into the end zone for a touchdown.

***

# Chapter 27
# Golden Opportunity

The 1990 season had me rolling in on a scholarship before half was mysteriously taken away. Internally, I absolutely dwelled on my situation every day. I knew in my heart that I could play fullback on game day at the Division I level. I felt I had proven that every day in practice and was absolutely steadfast in my belief. I also knew the defensive coaches loved having me on scout team because I tested their starters at the level of real game conditions, and I would not back down. I had received the Scout Team Player of thc Week award many times, but I expected, and demanded it of myself that I win it every week. I had hoped that if I kept winning the award the coaches would realize that I deserved to be promoted from Scout Team to running with the top fullbacks at the other end of the field.

In mid-November 1990, we played cross-town rival UCLA. While I traveled with the team, and started on all the special teams on Saturdays, I was still stuck practicing on scout team Monday through Thursday. I felt I had a dominating week of practice going against our starting defense. But, on the following Monday in our team meeting, I did not get the Scout Team Player of the Week

Award. I was pretty perturbed because I knew I had made more of an impact than anyone else that week in practice.

Frustrated, I walked straight into our linebacker coach Tom Roggeman's office after the meeting and sat down uninvited. "Coach, what did I do wrong this past week?"

He looked at me and said, "Lavin, what the hell are you talking about? You didn't do anything wrong. You were great, as always."

"Well, then why did I not win Scout Team Player of the Week? I dominated out there and you know I did because you yelled at your linebackers almost every play because I was getting the better of them," I stated emphatically.

Coach Roggeman leaned forward in his chair putting his elbows on his desk and said, "Lav, we can give you the Scout Team Award every week. But, we have to spread the wealth a little. We need to give confidence to some of the other guys."

I stood up, peered down at the coach, and told him, "I'm NOT a scout team lifer! If I deserve to be at the other end of the field with the starting offense, then that's where I should be!" Coach Roggeman just nodded his head in agreement and I walked out of his office.

Every time I climbed the ladder I felt I got knocked down. The fire burned deep inside me. Determined to stand out, be different, and make a statement, I looked for another way to get noticed. On that Monday after the UCLA game and preceding the Notre Dame contest of November 24, 1990, I saw something I had seen hundreds of times before but never took notice of it until that moment. It didn't mean anything to me for two and a half years, but I saw it screaming back at me that day. I was still livid from not getting the scout team award and my mind was racing. It was a San Francisco 49ers helmet hanging from the ceiling in the equipment room along with several other team helmets that our equipment manager, Dino Dennis, had collected over his long career. Managers would often swap swag in the form of collectors' items from opposing teams.

Zeroing in on the helmet, my mind was spinning. I thought that if I peeled off the 49er decals on the side of the helmet, and the stripes running down the center, I would be left with a gold looking helmet—the same look as the Fighting Irish. The Golden Dome helmet is as iconic a fixture to the Fighting Irish as Tommy Trojan and Traveler, the white horse, are to USC. Steeped in tradition, the gold helmet is a visual representation that emulates the Golden Dome overlooking the Irish football stadium. Knowing this, wearing the gold helmet in practice that week could be something special, something huge. I was lighting one enormous fuse.

As the scout team fullback, I would be wearing jersey number 5 in practice that week representing Notre Dame's fullback

Rodney Culver. Notre Dame was ranked sixth in the country (they had been ranked number 1 but lost to Colorado the week before our game and had dropped to six.) USC had started the season in the top 10, but we dropped to 18 by the ND game.

I asked Dino if I could take the helmet down, peel off all the stickers and wear it in practice. He thought it was a great idea and knew I was the type of player that was crazy enough to wear it, just to stir things up. While the idea was intriguing, he told me I'd have to get the approval of Coach Smith. Immediately reporting to the coach's office, I met with Smith and told him I had an idea to fire up the defense in practice. Surprisingly, he thought it was pretty creative and told me to go for it. Game on!

My goal was not entirely to fire up our defense. It was done more to get me noticed and be the focal point of our scrimmages that week. It was my way of showing the coaches I was different. Racing back downstairs to the equipment room, I told Dino we were good to go, and he handed me the helmet. We removed the stickers, and I put it on. Whoops! It was tight—really, really tight. Perhaps I should have tried it on before I had shared the idea. It fit, but it was like squeezing a size 12 foot into a size 11 shoe. You probably can do it, but it's going to be very uncomfortable.

Monday's practice was a no-contact day so I kept the gold helmet hidden in my locker in order not to reveal what I had up my sleeve for Tuesday and Wednesday's full contact practices. Other than Dino and Coach Smith, I told no one what I was doing. Not wearing full pads that day, we ran through the game plan for the week. We practiced the plays we would run offensively and our plan of how to stop the Irish defensively. We went over our special teams to end the day. That evening I went home and gave myself a buzz haircut in hopes of making the gold helmet a tad more tolerable to wear. I wasn't totally bald, but it looked like I had just joined the military.

This was another "statement moment" for me. I wanted to show the staff I was not just another walk-on who was content with only playing special teams on Saturday and being a practice player the rest of the week. I had to prove I could play fullback and go against one of the top defenses in the country and not only hold my own, but make an impact, especially during Notre Dame week.

On Tuesday, we were in full pads, and it was a full contact day with hard-nosed scrimmaging. It was my game day and I was pumped up. When we walked from the locker room to the practice field, we had to hit the grass at a jog and trot around the field with a warm-up lap. After pre-practice meetings, we had about a 20-minute window to get on the field before our practice officially got started with stretching exercises. During that 20-minute period, guys would be tossing the ball around, running patterns, and loosening up. On this day, I purposely delayed leaving the locker room and kept my gold helmet concealed in the locker until the last possible minute.

Being one of the last guys to hit the field before practice officially started allowed for the entire team and the coaching staff to be on the field already along with the media and special guests. With just a couple of minutes to spare before practice officially started I donned the gold helmet, secured the buckle, and bolted through the gate onto the field. I ran at top speed and was singing the Notre Dame Victory March fight song as loud as I could.

With fire in my belly and ready to rumble, I belted out: "Cheer, cheer for old Notre Dame, Wake up the echoes cheering her name, Send a volley cheer on high, Shake down the thunder from the sky. What though the odds be great or small, Old Notre Dame will win over all, While her loyal sons are marching Onward to victory."

For good measure, I repeated the song as I ran around the field. Everything and everyone on the field came to a screeching halt. My teammates stopped warming up, stretching, and running patterns. They stopped throwing and kicking balls. All stood still; I was the only thing moving as I circled the field in my golden dome helmet singing our opponents' fight song. As the players watched me run around the field the chatter and comments started flying my way. I was ready for a full on scrimmage right then and there.

A number of defensive players screamed out to me that I was “dead meat” come scrimmage time. They used some other choice language not seen on SAT tests explaining in so many words that the war was on and that they were going to kill me and rip my helmet off, etc. This was exactly the reaction I had expected and had wanted. I was too fired up to be scared, even though I knew it was going to be 11 against 1 when we started scrimmaging.

Contrary to the defensive players' reactions, the offensive players and kickers thought it was hysterical. Of course, they egged me on and screamed back to the defensive players that I was going to run them over in practice and destroy them. There was both laughter and tension in the air, and I was right smack in the middle of it. It was precisely what I had envisioned. Let’s get after it!

After our typical team stretching and individual drills, it was scrimmage time. The media and spectators were now at our end of the field for the first time all year.

Since offensive players typically get a majority of the press, the media and spectators during practice tend to hang out at the “offensive end” of the field. Normally, you could expect about 80 percent of people watching practice at the offensive end while about 20 percent would be watching the defensive starters.

On this day, however, and on the following day, about 80 percent of the media and spectators were hanging out at our end of the field to watch the starting defense against this psycho scout team offensive player donning a gold helmet. We did not disappoint.

There were plenty of fights, finger pointing, bottom of the pile pushing and shoving, and lots of jabbering directed at me. The kickers, punters, and long snappers stopped their individual drills and watched the scrimmage. They loved the banter and physical intensity, and they cheered me on from the sidelines. Several of them were walk-ons too and enjoyed seeing me succeed, play after play. They loved to antagonize the defense from afar and try to instigate more fights by yelling things like, "They can't stop you Lavin," and "Mad Dog is kicking your ass, defense!"

It was terrific entertainment for the spectators, and I was the focal point of almost every play—hitting people hard and making a statement. This lasted all day Tuesday and Wednesday. Thursday was a very light day, and Friday was just a walk-through of our assignments, so I gave the helmet back to Dino after Wednesday night's practice.

Unfortunately, we lost Saturday's game 10-6 at the L.A. Coliseum. But our defense played tough, giving up only 10 points against a high powered Notre Dame offense. However, the Notre Dame defense played equally well and only allowed two Trojan field goals. Regardless of the final outcome, it was a powerful showing by our defense.

When the weekly awards were given out the following Monday at our team meeting, my efforts were recognized and I received the Scout Team Player of the Week award. Did I play a role in preparing our defense to play well on that Saturday? We'll never know for sure, but I do know I made a statement. In any case, it enhanced my status, and I earned more respect by the coaching staff. I do believe it contributed to my playing time. I was already playing Saturdays on all the special teams that year, but I believe it set the tone for the following 1991 season, as I kept my spot on all the special teams, moved up to second team fullback, and was granted the full scholarship I had sought for three long years.

The Golden Dome helmet was an opportunity to put destiny in my own hands. I had nothing to lose and everything to gain.

***

## Golden Compliment

**Mike Garrett**

**1965 Heisman Trophy Winner**

Towards the end of my tenure at USC, 1965 Heisman Trophy winner Mike Garrett was working in the athletic building and eventually would become the Athletic Director in 1993. During my last couple of years, Garrett could be seen on our practice field observing the team. I never had the courage to go up and introduce myself to him after any of our practices. He was a Heisman Trophy winner, the greatest award in all of sports. He just seemed bigger than life to me and I was intimidated. I was too scared to bother him.

I assumed he knew who I was because the year before he was a TV commentator for Prime Ticket and actually did our Utah State game where I had two carries for 20 years and he was very complimentary of my ball carrying. That was pretty inspiring to hear him talk about me.

During my Golden Dome helmet wearing practice I noticed Mike Garrett watching me. Can you imagine my surprise and utter shock when Mr. Garrett approached me after practice before the ND game with the gold helmet in my hand and told me he thought I was one of the toughest players he has ever seen! He did not know I started off as a walk-on until later. But, he told me right then, "You are what USC football is all about."

We spoke many times after that encounter including an incredible experience I got to share with my brother, Jay. I had moved to the San Francisco Bay Area in the late 1990's. USC Head Coach Paul Hackett was in the middle of a speaking circuit around California to the different USC Alumni Groups. When I had heard Coach Hackett would be giving a speech in San Francisco, I called the Trojan Athletic Department in search of a couple tickets. The call I got back from USC floored me. The secretary told me that Mike Garrett had heard that I called and not only was he going to be San Francisco as well, but he wanted my brother and me to sit at his table. Are you kidding me? Wow!

Moving forward, Jay and I were thrilled to be going to the event and to be sitting at the table of a Heisman Trophy winner. When the evening started Mike Garrett took to the microphone and made his speech about USC and Trojan football. Before bringing up Head Coach Paul Hackett to speak, he wanted to recognize one more person in the room. Mr. Garrett proceeded to introduce me sitting at his table. He talked about my accomplishments, starting off as a walk-on, getting playing time on Saturdays, earning a scholarship and playing like a Trojan should. He finished his speech by saying the same words he said to me on the football field after my golden dome practice so many years before, "Tim Lavin is what USC football is all about." That was met with a huge ovation from the crowd as I sat in my chair in utter astonishment. I could not have been more surprised or honored.

When I called Mr. Garrett to tell him of this book I was writing about the world of walk-ons, he said; "…this is outstanding! America loves the underdog and they will rally behind you!" Now as Athletic Director of Langston University in

Oklahoma and after serving as AD at USC for nearly 18 years, Garrett does believe there needs to be a change in the system with regard to walk-ons. He, too, believes walk-ons should be allowed to eat at training-table without having to pay for it and he also believes a walk-on should not have to sit out a year if he decides to transfer. “The school is not invested in the player, so why should he suffer the penalty of transferring like a scholarship player would have to?”

My sentiments exactly. Thank you, Mr. Garrett!

***

# Chapter 28
# Hall of Fame Walk-Ons

So many people had something to say about this book. It was impossible to report everything without creating encyclopedic volumes. Rather than kicking so many great stories to the curb, I decided to list as many people as I could in the shortest amount of space.

In 2010, *Famous Football Walk-Ons* was published in *Sports Illustrated.* You might be surprised at some of the names after seeing them in the NFL for so many years. Being a walk-on is just not something that is talked about much once you make it. Here is the *Sports Illustrated* list:

**Brandon Burlsworth – Arkansas**
A walk-on for the Arkansas Razorbacks in 1996, Burlsworth eventually became a second-team All-America and a third-round pick of the Indianapolis Colts.
(Tragically, eleven days after being drafted, he was killed in a car accident.)

**Karl Mecklenburg - Minnesota**
A walk-on at Minnesota, Mecklenburg went on to become a two-time second-team All-Big Ten selection and a 12th round pick of the Denver Broncos. With Denver, the defensive lineman once again beat the odds by playing his way to six Pro Bowls and three Super Bowl appearances.

**Louis Oliver - Florida**

After graduating from Glades Central High School in Belle Glade, Fla., Oliver walked on to Galen Hall's Florida Gators squad in 1985. From there, Oliver earned an athletic scholarship, became a starting free safety and team captain for the Gators and was a first-team All-America selection in 1987 and 1988.

**Aeneas Williams – Southern University**

Williams is a unique addition to this list as the sole walk-on who wasn't itching to get on the gridiron. He didn't take up football until his junior year at Southern University but by his senior year he had tied the Division 1-AA single-season record with 11 interceptions.

**Darren Woodson - Arizona State**

A walk-on linebacker at Arizona State, Woodson was named to five Pro Bowls and went on to win three Super Bowls with the Dallas Cowboys. Woodson is just one of several Sun Devils who went from walk-on to NFL pro (Adam Archuleta and Levi Jones also accomplished the feat).

**Andre Wadsworth - Florida State**

Lightly recruited out of high school, Andre Wadsworth decided to walk on at Florida State in 1994. Despite playing tight end in high school, Wadsworth played defensive tackle for the Seminoles and earned All-ACC honors during his freshman, sophomore, junior and senior years.

**Scott Fujita – California**

Though recruited by several Ivy League schools, Fujita opted to walk on at the University of California, Berkeley in 1997. Originally a safety, Fujita made the seamless transition to collegiate linebacker and earned a scholarship shortly thereafter.

**Santana Moss – Miami**
A walk-on for the Miami Hurricanes in 1997, Moss would graduate as the school's leader in receiving yards (2,546) and all-purpose yards (4,393).

**Gary Brackett – Rutgers**
Brackett walked on to the Scarlet Knights in 1999. He played sparingly, mostly on special teams, but showed enough for Rutgers to offer him a scholarship during his sophomore year. By the time Brackett was a senior, he was the Scarlet Knights' captain and led the team with 130 tackles, second-most in the Big East that year.

**Colt Brennan - Hawaii**
Colt Brennan is another rarity in that he walked on twice, first at the University of Colorado in 2003, then again in 2005 at the University of Hawaii. His second stint proved more successful, and by the time Brennan graduated in 2008 he held the NCAA record for most touchdown passes in a single season, highest pass completion percentage and passing efficiency.

**Logan Mankins - Fresno State**
A walk-on at Fresno State, Mankins started 14 games as a redshirt freshman, allowing only two sacks on future No. 1 pick, David Carr. He was named to the Freshman All-America team and would later become the first offensive lineman in Fresno State history to win the team's MVP award.

**Jordy Nelson - Kansas State**
The Manhattan, Kansas. native walked on at Kansas State and drew national attention during his sophomore campaign when he caught 45 passes and 8 touchdowns. Injuries largely derailed Nelson's junior season, but he showed his

stats weren't a fluke when he caught 122 passes for 1,606 yards and 11 touchdowns during his senior season with the Wildcats.

**Clay Matthews - USC**
Thought to be too small and too slow to play at the collegiate level, Matthews walked on at USC in 2004 largely because of who his father was. Matthews didn't earn a scholarship until 2006 and didn't start until his senior year, but he showed enough to warrant a first-round pick from the Green Bay Packers. The definition of a late bloomer, Matthews has 22.0 career sacks in just two NFL seasons.

Speaking of Clay Matthews: Clay was 6'1," 165 lbs coming out of high school. He had no Division I offers and Junior College seemed like the logical choice if he wanted to keep playing football. But, with walk-ons, what is logical to you may not be logical to a walk-on. Clay's father played at USC and spent 19 years in the NFL. Head Coach Pete Carroll, who loves walk-ons and will take them all day long, was brutally honest with Clay's father and told him his son would never play at USC and if he wanted to play college football to go to a Division II or Division III school. Clay looked his father in the eye and said he would prove Coach Carroll wrong.

He lived in the weight room and became a walk-on at USC in 2004. Two years later in 2006, Clay Matthews was running around the game day field on special teams after earning a scholarship.

In 2006 and 2007, Clay continued to dominate on Special Teams and was a reserve linebacker. But, by 2008, his senior year, Matthews was starting and wrecking havoc on opposing defenses and quarterbacks. Clay Matthews was drafted in the first round of the 2009 NFL Draft by the Green Bay Packers. Two seasons into his NFL career, Clay was a Super Bowl Champion.

Not to be outdone by *Sports Illustrated*, *CBSSports.com* came out with an All-Decade Walk-On Team in 2013. Here is the CBS Sports article:

**All-Walk-On Team: The decade's most surprising successes**

People who make their living sizing up high school recruits for the next level overwhelmingly know what they're doing: Coaches who pass on future stars while handing out scholarships to future busts tend not to last very long. And even the online recruiting rankings, when taken as a whole, have a consistent track record of predicting who's going to make it and who's not. The conventional wisdom about what makes (or breaks) a viable college player is conventional for a reason.

And then, inevitably, every so often it is dead wrong. With another signing day in the books and all but a few available scholarships off the table; here's a brief reminder from the past decade of the undersized, overlooked and scholarship-lacking walk-ons who came out on top despite initially falling through the cracks. All of the following players saw the field within the last 10-12 years, but none of them were considered worthy of a scholarship at the FBS level -- until they showed up on campus and earned it the hard way.

**Quarterback: COLT BRENNAN** Hawaii
Brennan actually walked on twice: First at Colorado, where he was eventually dismissed amid many wrong doings, and later at Hawaii, where coach June Jones decided to give Brennan a second chance after stumbling across his junior college film while scouting another player. Three years later, Brennan left the islands on the heels of the best season in school history with NCAA records for passing yards, completion percentage and efficiency in a career.

**Running Back: CHAD SPANN** Northern Illinois
He's easy to overlook in a long line of productive NIU workhorses, but the diminutive Spann made his mark with a pair of 1,000-yard campaigns in 2009 and 2010, earning first-team All-MAC honors both years as the engine of the best ground attack in the league. He led the nation as a senior with 22 touchdowns.

**Fullback: Owen Schmitt** West Virginia
Before he famously bloodies himself up for the NFL crowd, Schmitt was immortalized in the 2008 Fiesta Bowl as the "Runaway Beer Truck," a fitting tag for a career spent flattening things in service of one of the most feared offenses in the country. Despite his reputation as a blocker, Schmitt began his college career as a 1,000-yard rusher at a Division III school, Wisconsin-River Falls, and ended it with nearly 1,300 total yards and 15 touchdowns in three years as a Mountaineer. (Just please, for his own sake, don't ask him to punt.)

**Wide Receiver: PATRICK EDWARDS** Houston
For Edwards, in retrospect, getting on the field *sans* scholarship was the easy part. The hard part was getting *back* on the field after suffering a grisly broken leg on national television in 2008. From there, Edwards returned to haul in 291 receptions over the next three years for more yards (4,507) and touchdowns (43) than any other receiver in college football in that span, and was rewarded as a senior by being named Conference USA's Offensive Player of the Year.

**Wide Receiver: MIKE HASS** Oregon State
Hass broke into the Beavers' receiving rotation as a sophomore in 2003 and proceeded to establish himself as one of the most quietly reliable receivers in the Pac-10, turning in three consecutive 1,000-yard seasons in an offense better known at the time for producing prolific tailbacks. By his senior year in 2005, the secret was out; Hass went over 100 yards receiving in 9 of 11 games, and multiple outlets made him a first-team All-American.

**Wide Receiver: JORDY NELSON** Kansas State
His subsequent success at the next level has made the scouts' indifference toward Nelson that much harder to grasp. But even K-State fans had to be taken by surprise when Nelson made the leap from solid-but-unspectacular role player to consensus All-American as a senior, setting school records for catches (122), yards (1,606) and touchdowns (11) in the process. He still ranks second in Wildcat history by all three measures.

**Tight End: DENNIS PITTA** BYU
Pitta was the only former walk-on in either starting lineup in Sunday's Super Bowl, which will come as no surprise to anyone who followed his All-America career at BYU. Over

four years in Provo, Pitta set the school record for receptions (221). The Cougars landed in the final Top 25 all four years.

**Ofensive Line: LEVY ADCOCK** Oklahoma State
Adcock never had a chance of stealing the spotlight from the walk-on quarterback whom he protected, Brandon Weeden, but he was every bit as integral to Oklahoma State's emergence as a perennial offensive juggernaut, starting 26 consecutive games at both left and right tackle with a pair of first-team All-Big 12 nods after transferring from Northeastern Oklahoma A&M. He went out in 2011 as a consensus All-American on a team that came within inches of playing for the national championship.

**Offensive Line: LOGAN MANKINS** Fresno State
Before he was an iron man for the New England Patriots, Mankins was a rock up front for Fresno State, starting every game in both 2001 and 2002, then returning from an ACL injury that cost him all of 2003 to start every game in 2004. He didn't allow a sack that year, was voted first-team All-WAC and went off the board in the first round the following April. Before he hurt his leg last December, Mankins hadn't missed an NFL start to injury in nearly eight full seasons.

**Offensive Line: RYLAN REED** Texas Tech
If he'd never set foot on the field, there'd still be plenty to say about Reed, a former minor league pitcher who beat cancer and reportedly bench-pressed 625 pounds. (According to Reed's o-line coach at Tech, "It's almost like he plays football so he can work out.") But it turns out Reed was actually kind of good at football, too, eventually earning first-team All-Big 12 and All-America honors in 2008 as an immovable left tackle on the best team in school history.

**Offensive Line: RICKY WAGNER** Wisconsin
A dozen Wisconsin offensive linemen have been drafted in the last dozen years -- 300-pound behemoths are the state's leading export, in fact; -- but when Wagner goes off the board this April, he'll be the first who arrived in Madison without a scholarship since Mark Tauscher went to the Green Bay Packers in the seventh round in 2000. Wagner leaves with 38 starts over the last three years for teams that steamrolled their way into three consecutive Rose Bowls and as the best example yet that the Badgers can basically stumble across All-Big Ten blockers without even trying.

**Center: SEAN BEDFORD** Georgia Tech
As a center, Bedford was a two-time All-ACC pick, starting 27 consecutive games as the anchor of the prolific triple-option attack that carried the 2009 Yellow Jackets to their first conference championship in nearly two decades. As an aerospace engineering major, he's also a rocket scientist. When we come back: Precision cut blocks on Mars.

**Defensive Line: IAN CAMPBELL** Kansas State
K-State is a perennial pipeline for the overlooked. But even by Wildcat standards, Campbell was an obscurity, walking on in 2004 from a tiny town of barely 2,000 people. From there, he grew into a three-time All-Big 12 pick by league coaches as both a linebacker and a defensive end and lives on on YouTube for the time that he was caught on film clearing a 62-inch hurdle.

**Defensive Line: MARGUS HUNT** SMU
A former discus champion from Estonia, Hunt originally enrolled at SMU in 2007 to work with women's track coach, Dave Wollman, a renowned throwing expert who was attempting to revive the school's defunct men's team. When that effort fell through Wollman pointed Hunt in the direction

of June Jones, who took one look at the 6‘ 7”, 280-pound hulk in a tryout and put him on scholarship before he had played a single snap of organized football. Five years later, Hunt is leaving as a first-team All-Conference USA pick and a likely 2nd or 3rd rounder in April's draft.

**Defensive Line: J.J. WATT** Wisconsin
Watt is an exception here; the only player on this list who actually began his college career on scholarship: As an unheralded, 220-pound tight end at Central Michigan. After a single season in the MAC, though, he returned to his home state to walk on with the Badgers, (who molded him into a 280-pound All-American, first-round draft pick and all-purpose wrecking ball on the defensive line), Watt is recognized as arguably the best defensive player in the NFL and the inspiration behind at least one bizarre wedding cake.

**Defensive Line: RYAN WINTERSWYK** Boise State
Most of the credit for Boise's ascent went to the ultra-efficient offense, but the defense also ranked among the nation's best during Winterswyk's tenure, which spanned the Broncos' insurgent 38-2 run from 2008-2010. Initially pegged as a safety, Winterswyk emerged instead as a cornerstone on the line, where he led the team in tackles for loss as a Redshirt freshman and earned All-WAC nods from opposing coaches three years in a row.

**Linebacker: GARY BRACKET** Rutgers
Before he picked up a Super Bowl ring with the Indianapolis Colts, Brackett picked up team MVP honors at Rutgers in 2002 after leading the team with 130 tackles as a senior. The Scarlet Knights went 1-11 that season, Greg Schiano's second as head coach, made Brackett one of the last players to escape the black hole that was Rutgers football before Schiano's rebuilding effort finally took root. He might

also be the only author to actually incorporate the term "walk-on" into a book title.

**Linebacker: CLAY MATTHEWS** USC
Matthews has not always cut the Herculean figure that he currently exploits on TV. In high school, his father, a longtime NFL linebacker, turned defensive coordinator, considered his son too small to start until he was a senior. College scouts agreed. At his dad's alma mater Matthews found a niche on special teams but didn't crack the regular starting lineup until his senior year, 2008, when a unit loaded with future NFL talent led the nation in scoring defense en route to USC's sixth consecutive Pac-10 title. Of the dozen Trojans eventually drafted off that defense, only Matthews and fellow linebacker Brian Cushing went in the first round.

**Linebacker: DARYL WASHINGTON** TCU
He doesn't have the pedigree or the profile, media-wise, but the trajectory of Washington's career has been strikingly similar to Matthews'. Like Matthews, Washington was overlooked by scouts after starting only one season in high school; like Matthews, he spent most of his time on campus as a backup on a series of first-rate defenses. When he finally cracked the lineup as a senior in 2009, Washington was an instant hit, picking up a handful of All-America notices as the leading tackler on the No. 1 total defense in the nation; TCU finished the regular season 12-0 and entered the Fiesta Bowl ranked No. 3. And, like Matthews, Washington has justified his high draft status by emerging as one of the best young linebackers in the league.

**Cornerback: KEVIN ARBET** USC
Arbet is not destined to go down as one of the great Trojan talents of the Pete Carroll era, but he did start 12 games in 2003 and 2004 for teams that spent a combined 18 weeks at

the top of the Associated Press Poll, making him the only player on this list to start on a team that claimed a national championship, disputed, vacated or otherwise. Before his move into the starting lineup, Arbet also returned kicks and was a first-team All-Pac-10 pick in 2001 as a Special-Teams player.

**Cornerback: IKE TAYLOR** Louisiana-Lafayette
Taylor is another late bloomer, forced to sit out his first two years at UL-Lafayette due to academics and then relegated to a backup role as tailback as a junior. It was only after he requested a move to cornerback for his senior season that he found his niche on defense, starting every game opposite Charles "Peanut" Tillman in 2002. From there, Taylor's blazing speed at the NFL Combine led to a fourth-round flier from the Pittsburgh Steelers, where he remains one decade and two Super Bowl rings later.

**Safety: RASHAD JOHNSON** Alabama
Farfetched as it seems when contemplating Alabama's fully Sabanized depth chart in 2013, it was still possible for a walk-on to break through in Saban's first two seasons, 2007 and 2008, when Johnson started every game and led the Tide in tackles and interceptions both years. As a senior, Johnson was voted first-team All-SEC by league coaches and landed on a pair of All-America teams, while the Saban era began in earnest with a 12-0 regular season.

**Safety: JIM LEONHARD** Wisconsin
Poster child for the undersized and overlooked, Leonhard set the standard for Big Ten safeties from 2002-2004, tying a school record for career interceptions (21) en route to First-Team All-conference honors -- and at least one All-America nod -- in all three seasons. He also set a Big Ten mark for punt return yards in a career (since broken by Michigan's

Steve Breaston), taking three punts to the house for touchdowns. Ignored again by NFL scouts, Leonhard just wrapped up his eighth season in the league with his fourth team.

***HONORABLE MENTION:***
**WR *Jared Abbrederis*, Wisconsin … LB *Ezekiel Ansah*, BYU … WR *Antonio Brown*, Central Michigan … QB *Austin Davis*, Southern Miss … OL *B.J. Finnie*, Kansas State … LB *Josh Hull*, Penn State … S *Jordan Kovacs*, Michigan … OL *Spencer Long*, Nebraska … QB *Bryant Moniz*, Hawaii … WR *Tommy Saunders*, Missouri … QB *Brandon Weeden*, Oklahoma State … WR *Ryan Whalen*, Stanford.**

**So Many More Deserving**

Let it be known there are scores of other incredible walk-ons who deserve to be listed right here. Time and space were the enemy, but I will keep a running list on the Walk-OnU.com website and I fully intend the sequel to this book will show an even greater list of compelling walk-ons and their life changing stories.

A few of my personal favorites, some known, some lesser known, but should be known:

**The Son of a Preacher Man…**

Oren O'Neal was sitting with the church band strumming his guitar leading the choir in song. His father was the preacher.

Every Sunday was the all-important day for his family to sit amongst the congregation and give thanks to the good Lord above for their countless blessings.

On that Sunday, April 29, 2007, over 1,000 miles from where the young man sat in church playing his guitar, an announcement was made. "And with the First pick, in the 6th Round of the 2007 NFL Draft, the Oakland Raiders select, Oren O'Neal, Fullback, Arkansas State!"

Sitting in church O'Neal's cell phone was buzzing in his pocket. He let it go to voicemail not thinking much of the call. After realizing his phone would not stop buzzing he finally looked at it. He had missed calls from the Oakland Raiders, his agent, and numerous friends. It wasn't until after church that he received official word he had been drafted to play football in the NFL.

As a high school senior, O'Neal played both offensive and defensive line. When no scholarship offers came in he decided to walk-on at Arkansas State. During his freshman year he was having trouble breathing. He was checked out by the doctors and diagnosed with chylothorax, a lymphatic fluid (chyle) accumulating in the pleural cavity. As a result, part of his left lung was removed. He spent 21 days in the hospital. Some people would just be happy to be alive and be able to breathe. O'Neal wanted to play football again.

He had to sit out the entire next season because of his medical condition and he spent it in the weight room getting stronger! However, the bills were building up and he lost his apartment. He would sleep on floors and couches of fellow teammates. His scholarship brothers also bought him food on their meal cards. He needed to eat.

O'Neil was moved to fullback from offensive lineman and things started to click. He moved up the depth chart until he could not go any higher. He was first string. Head Coach Steve Roberts called O'Neil into his office. And then he called O'Neil's father on the telephone to explain his son and just earned a full scholarship.

A torn ACL knee injury cut short his professional career after just three short years with the Oakland Raiders organization. But, I think of a young man who walked-on a football team, had to share a locker, no name on the back of his jersey (like the scholarship players), got left over equipment and used cleats, lost the ability to breathe properly, spent three weeks in the hospital, was told he should retire, moved to fullback and had to learn a whole new position, beat out the rest and started for three years straight. The NCAA granted him a medical redshirt giving him one extra year eligibility since he had to sit out his redshirt freshman year allowing him to come back for a sixth year of college. Not only did he start for the fourth consecutive year, he earned two degrees in technical studies and industrial engineering!

He knew he did very well during his 6th season and excelled during the Pro Day testing in early spring. Yet, being with family in church was the most important thing in the world, even if the NFL Draft was going on. A focused walk-on with priorities.

***

**Mike Sherrard, Wide Receiver**

**UCLA**

**1981 – 1985**

It is very rare that a first round draft NFL selection (18th overall) started his career as an unrecruited stroll-on. That is how his former coach Homer Smith referred to Mike Sherrard, as a stroll-on. Sherrard had excellent grades in high school and was given the opportunity to excel in his studies at UCLA. He even wanted a head-start in his studies by enrolling in summer school. That's when something magical happened.

While walking to a summer school class Mike Sherrard saw some of the football players playing catch on the practice field. He stopped and peered through the metal bars and watched. He zeroed in on the wide receivers and he didn't care about being late for class. He realized he could play football with these guys. He asked a coach if he could tryout and the next day he was playing catch with the team. It was obvious Mike could catch the ball and the coaches invited him to walk-on in the fall.

Being a walk-on meant that Mike had to pay for everything so he held down two jobs. He was selling tennis shoes at Big 5 Sporting Goods and then the athletic department got Mike another job, in the maintenance department and assigned him to Pauley Pavilion, home to the Bruins' basketball and volleyball teams. While the student body rocked the house that John Wooden built, Mike was on the outside scrubbing walls and chipping off old paint.

His focus was on academics, making money to pay his bills, and football. After every great catch he made, Coach Homer Smith would yell out; "WOW, get that kid a scholarship!" By Seasons end Head Coach Terry Donahue granted Sherrard a full scholarship and Mike was able to retire from his odd jobs. As a sophomore in 1983, Sherrard was All Pac-10 and 3rd Team All-American. Injuries slowed his stats down as a junior and senior, but there was no doubt of what he could do when healthy. As a result, the Dallas Cowboys selected Mike Sherrard with the 18th pick in the first round and the former unrecruited walk-on went on to have an 11 year NFL career!

***

**Rich Coady, Safety**

**Texas A&M**

**1994 - 1998**

Rich Coady played eight years in the NFL. As a walk-on at Texas A&M, he was without a number, no logo on his helmet, and sporting a blue scout team jersey and told to hold a blocking bag. As Coady practiced and observed his competition at safety he knew he could work his way up the depth chart. In fact when the coaches realized they had to play him it happened so quickly they misspelled his last name on his game jersey and his name was not even in the program. The announcer just kept saying; "Tackle by number 48...(silence)…of the Aggies."

Coady was playing safety and special teams on Saturday, but still had to pay for his training table meals during the week. That was frustrating! But, he continued his mission and excelled!

Coady was selected in the 3rd Round of the 1999 NFL Draft by the Rams and won a Super Bowl in his rookie season. He went to play eight seasons in the National Football League.

## Big in Business

You don't have to play in the NFL to be a Hall of Fame Walk-On. Some walk-ons excel at the college level and then transfer their skills to the working world and make it big. Here are just two examples of walk-ons who rose to the top of their profession.

Perhaps you have heard of **Under Armour**, a leading manufacturer of sports performance apparel, footwear and accessories. Yes? Kevin Plank, a walk-on football player at the University of Maryland and special teams captain started the company in his grandmothers basement. The idea was to get rid of the soaking wet tee shirts worn during practice and replace it with a moisture wicking material that would keep athletes cool, dry and light.

Founded in 1996, Plank propelled the business year after year and the sports industry took notice. Under Armour had revenue of over $1.83 Billion in 2012. Now that is a walk-on success story.

***

I was able to speak with another walk-on who rose to the top. Meet Bill Emerson:

**Wild Bill's Pay Off**

You don't accidently become chief executive officer of Quicken Loans Inc., the nation's largest online home loan lender and third largest retail mortgage lender, with a half-hearted effort. You have to be different and willing to pay the price no matter what.

Bill Emerson walked-on to the Penn State football field in 1981. He was recruited to walk-on by many small schools, several

Ivy League institutions including Princeton, Lehigh, Cornell, Dartmouth, and Colgate as well as Penn State University. While the Ivy schools, especially Colgate, seemed tempting, Bill Emerson knew that if he was going to play football as a walk-on, he was going to do it at the largest school to show what he could do and became a Penn State Nittany Lion.

He endured the pummeling hits and punishing blows his walk-on freshman year from the upper classmen. But after the first two weeks, Bill decided he was going to turn it up and start dishing it out too. As a running back he was practicing against one of the best defenses in the country. He realized he could not just go through the motions on his athletic ability alone. He had to be different, work harder than everyone else, and be a force to be reckoned with. Respect was earned from his teammates, he fed off the adulation he received and never looked back.

His stock rose and so did his position. A great spring practice his freshman year catapulted him to run with the first group on Special Teams allowing him to start his entire sophomore season. Hc was MVP of Spring Practice before his junior season and received a full football scholarship along with a new nickname, "Wild Bill." By his senior year, Bill Emerson was captain of the Special Teams.

After his final year, Coach Joe Paterno offered to pay for a master's degree if Bill came back to be a Graduate Assistant

Coach. Bill Emerson turned him down. He wanted to take all that he had learned from his college experience and see what he could do in the next phase of his life in the "real world." With each endeavor he faced he poured his heart and soul in to it and was determined to work the hardest. He realized from his early walk-on days playing football that it's not always the most talented or the smartest guys that succeed, it's the guys that out work everyone else. He was determined to do that in the business world and he climbed the corporate ladder in rapid succession.

Wild Bill's work ethic took him to Penn State as a walk-on, earned him a scholarship, and enabled him to become a team captain. Using his walk-on skills and honing them for the boardroom, Captain Wild Bill evolved into Bill Emerson, CEO of Quicken Loans, one of the leading home loan lenders in the United States.

***

## Half Brothers

**Marc Preston 1987 – 1989**
**Marc Raab 1987 – 1991**
**Grant Runnerstrum 1989 – 1990**

A few of my teammates got the half scholarship deal too. Our punter, Marc Preston, and Long Snapper, Marc Raab both received half scholarships even though they had been starters for two years. Our kicker, Grant Runnerstrum, was our starting kicker for two seasons and was offered a half scholarship for his final spring semester. Frustrated, he pleaded his case to the athletic director and he was granted a full scholarship for his graduating semester.

A few players I bumped into along my journey who would not take NO for an answer.

**Lang Campbell, QB**
**William & Mary**
**2000 – 2004**

Walk-On Lang Campbell became a two year starter at quarterback and winner of the 2004 Walter Payton Award for most outstanding player in 1-AA football. Campbell threw for 6,494 passing yards during his career with 54 touchdowns.

**Aaron Gideon, Center**
**UCLA**
**1988 - 1992**

Aaron Gideon was a walk-on football player at UCLA on the offensive line. There was little money for school tuition so Gideon had to live at his parents' home and drive 45 minutes each way on the LA freeways. He routinely would have to scour his car for loose change so he could put in just enough gas to make it home or to school. The stress was high enough fighting to earn a scholarship let alone hoping he had enough fuel to get to his destination.

He won the starting center job. Then he broke his finger on his snapping hand. Keeping a low profile and his pain in check, he taught himself to snap the ball with four fingers. He didn't want to lose his job over a broken finger.

Gideon earned his scholarship, and was named the Bruins' Team Captain and Most Valuable Senior Offensive Player in 1992 after starting for three seasons.

**David Langolis**
**University of Southern California**
**1979 – 1982**

Dave Langolis was told by a Trojan coach they were 'good to go' and they didn't need him. He went to see Head Coach John Robinson in his office but was stopped by staff members and turned away. He stood outside the door every morning when they arrived for work, but was told, "No Thanks." Finally, he rushed past the secretary and went straight to Coach Robinson's office and demanded he get a shot. Robinson took one look at Langolis and said, "I love your enthusiasm. Report to Jack Ward in the medical room downstairs for a physical." He was given old equipment and told to hit the field.

Within weeks his teammates were screaming things like, "look at Wally Walk-On running over Chipper Dipper," referring to linebacker Chip Banks who was an All-American and went on to a stellar Pro-Bowl NFL career. Langolis made his way on to the game day field. Any when John Robinson took the Head Coaching position with the Los Angeles Rams, he requested David Langolis to come play for him. Langolis was drafted in the USFL and in his first game had 12 tackles. Six knee operations prohibited a long professional career. He earned a scholarship and played professionally because he would not take NO for an answer.

## For the Love of the Walk-On

Today, when you watch college football players on TV, one should wonder how many guys are playing for the true love of the game. How many are only playing because their God-given athletic ability got them a scholarship and a free college education? How many guys are just using college football as a stepping stone to the NFL?

When you watch a college football game, one thing is absolutely for sure. If you see or hear about a walk-on playing on Saturday, you know he is 100 percent playing for the true love of the game. Not that the scholarship guys don't have a love for the game. Most do. But many will tell you that, if they did not have a scholarship, they would not be out there busting their tail to be on the football team.

That is why it is beautiful to watch teams like Army, Navy, and Air Force play on Saturday. Those guys are playing for the true love of the game. Why? Because they're not thinking "my next stop is the NFL!" For many of those players, their next stop is Afghanistan.

Walk-ons play for the true love of the game. You have to just sit back and admire it. It is pure. The athletic department is not paying for their tuition, books, or room and board. No agent is illegally calling or knocking on their door to give them cash. Walk-ons are completely on their own, forking over tons of money to the institution, giving up scores of hours from other activities including study, social, and free time for the true love of the game. It is their opportunity to make an impact, and the internal proof they can make something of themselves by starting at the bottom and fighting their way up the ladder.

Coaches catch lightning in a jug when they recognize those special walk-ons who not only have talent but also bring that unparalleled "walk-on" factor to the team. It is a precious gift to have on your squad to help build up all players.

***

# Chapter 29

# Coaches Corner

## Tom Osborne: Nebraska Walk-Ons

When you think of the best walk-on programs in the country over the last several decades, there is one school that will not only be part of the discussion, but they will inarguably be rated number 1. The University of Nebraska and the name Tom Osborne will be at the top of every list in any debate.

Coach Osborne was the Athletic Director for the University of Nebraska when I reached out to him on June 4th, 2010, in hopes that he would take my call. I spoke to his assistant, Anne, and explained who I was and that I wanted to interview Coach Osborne for my *Walk-On U* book. She stated how incredibly busy he was and how this was not the best time for an interview.

She was right. What I did not know, what no one knew, was that Nebraska was about to make a major announcement about jumping conferences just one week later. That news hit the airwaves June 10th, 2010:

***On June 10, 2010 ESPN News Reported:***
*A source close to the Nebraska program told ESPN's Chris Mortensen that athletic director Tom Osborne informed some staff members within the past 24 hours the*

*Cornhuskers were going to make the move to the Big Ten Conference.*

Let's back up one week to June 4th. On that Friday I had my conversation with Coach Osborne's assistant, Anne. She explained to me this was not a good time for the interview since Coach Osborne's schedule was jam-packed. Since I was unaware of the major announcement that was going to be made a week later, I gently persisted. I asked Anne if I could send her a one-page query letter about the book so she could pass it on to Coach Osborne. Basically, I begged her with all of my charm to show it to him. I said, "If he does not have time now, but wants to schedule an interview sometime in the future, then so be it. If he throws it in the trash, que sera sera." She replied that she would give it to him but, cautioned that I probably would not be hearing from him in the near future. She obviously knew the big news on the horizon and was aware that an interview with an unknown would not land high on his priority list. However, we are talking about Coach Tom Osborne, pioneer of the Walk-On Program. So, I held out hope.

My query letter was sent to Anne on Friday, June 4, 2010. On Monday morning, June 7th, I received this email:

***Sent:*** *Monday, June 07, 2010 8:41 AM*
***To:*** *Tim Lavin*
***Subject:*** *RE: Walk-On Through to the Other Side*

*Dear Tim,*
*I would be glad to speak with you on the phone regarding walk-ons or would be happy to answer some questions via e-mail regarding the same topic.*
*Thanks for writing.*
*Best wishes,*
*Tom Osborne*

I was thrilled and immediately wrote back and Anne replied that she would call me at 2:30 Pacific Standard Time later that afternoon. Like a little kid on Christmas morning I anxiously paced my office walking circles around the phone waiting for it to ring. At precisely 2:30 p.m. the phone rang and it was Anne. She stated she would put Coach Osborne on the phone, but warned me, again, that it would be a short call due to his hectic schedule; perhaps five minutes.

Coach Osborne got on the line and I was now talking to one of the legendary coaches in all of sports. I was both nervous and excited. Realizing his brief time for my call, I quickly peppered him with an overall synopsis of the book. He explained the walk-on program at Nebraska. Five minutes turned to ten, ten turned to twenty, and then at the 29 minute mark we finally ended our call. It was amazing! He did not have to take this interview, especially in light of the huge press release about to hit the newswires just three days in the future. But, since he did take the interview, he could have kept the call at five minutes like Anne had stated. Yet, he graciously stayed on the phone for nearly a half an hour. Here was a man about to make a major move in college football taking his football program from the Big 12 to the Big 10 Conference and yet he paused long enough to do an interview with me! Why? Because that is how incredibly important walk-ons are to him, and the football program at Nebraska!

**The Secret**

In Coach Tom Osborne's very early days of coaching he experienced a situation that left a powerful impression on him. The team practiced at a field almost a mile from the school. A bus would shuttle the players back and forth; except, the bus was for scholarship players only. When Coach Osborne first saw the walk-ons walking back to school after a long practice, his heart dropped. He recalled the situation being so dehumanizing and disrespectful that it was painful for him to observe and his heart was bleeding.

On that day he made a promise to himself, and every future walk-on he would ever coach for his lifetime, that under his tutelage no walk-on would ever be disrespected. That promise would lead him to have the most powerful walk-on program in the country as the head coach at the University of Nebraska for 25 years, and it still holds true today!

His secret was quite simple and so commonsensical it is truly a wonder why everyone does not follow these basic principles today. Some do, but most don't. Those that do, get the best walk-ons. Maybe one day every school in the country will subscribe to the Tom Osborne walk-on philosophy.

So, what is this great secret? First, Coach Osborne would make sure every player, scholarship or walk-on, was treated the same. From the top down and the bottom up, everyone treated everyone with respect! In fact, most scholarship players didn't even know who the walk-ons were unless they asked them point-blank.

Next, everyone gets a shot. He never made promises he could not keep. He did not guarantee scholarship players that they would be the starter, but he did guarantee they would have to fight for their starting position. He also gave everyone a chance to prove themselves on the field, including walk-ons. He made sure the walk-ons got a fair shake; an opportunity to prove they were worthy of playing on Saturdays.

Thirdly, he dangled the carrots. He made a promise to the walk-ons that if they worked their way up to number one or two on the depth chart by fall training camp they would automatically earn that coveted scholarship. Every year Coach Osborne would hold back several scholarships during the high school recruiting trail and save them for the walk-ons he knew were on the cusp of breaking into the top 1 or 2 positions on the depth chart. And every year several walk-ons earned their stripes and Coach Osborne kept his promises.

So, that's it? Yes! That's it! Treat all players the same and with respect. Give everyone a fair chance to make the most of their opportunity. And if they earn it, give them the scholarship, period.

While this sounds so simple, it is not and here's why. Unfortunately, too many coaches, equipment managers, trainers, and other athletic department personnel put scholarship players on pedestals. In their eyes walk-ons are typically located just above dirt level. As a result it is very difficult for them to treat these two entities with equal respect. It is sad, but true.

Unfortunately, there are still too many coaches out there who suffer from the "Walk-On Syndrome." They believe that all or almost all walk-ons are sub-par athletes. They also believe that there is no way that a walk-on could possibly be better than the guy they recruited. They spent so much time, energy, and money recruiting some great athlete and gave him a scholarship. And then some no-name "walk-on" comes in and beats his guy out?! That's a bitter pill for a lot of coaches to swallow. It's a pride thing. It's a stubborn thing. It's a personal thing. It's an embarrassing thing if the walk-on beats out the guy they recruited at great time, evaluation and expense. Therefore, most walk-ons don't get the chance to beat out the scholarship guys. The immature coach with too much pride will make sure of that.

Unfortunately (again), too many coaches believe in the hostage theory. In other words, even if a walk-on has proven himself to be worthy of a scholarship they won't give it to him because they feel he has the means to pay for his tuition and they can use that scholarship for the next high school kid. So, in essence they don't reward the deserving player, they just pat him on the back real hard. Or, disgracefully, if a walk-on deserves a scholarship and gets one because it is available, the coach could rip it out from under his feet if they need it later on. Yes, that has happened – embarrassingly! Absolutely astonishing!

Or, the coaches don't have enough discipline to hold back some scholarships and they offer all of them to high school and junior college transfers. If a coaching staff has 25 scholarships in hand, they give out 25 scholarships. Coach Osborne's theory was to only give out 21 or 22 scholarships and keep the rest for his most deserving walk-ons. That's the difference.

It's funny, even with all these tips from the master Coach Osborne, many, perhaps most, coaches won't implement them into their own programs or they will just carry out one or two of these tips and expect miracles. It's so interesting how a little respect, opportunity, and healthy competition can be so very rewarding in the end for the walk-ons, the staff, and the team.

Sure, one could argue that Coach Osborne had a little advantage in that many born and bred football players from Nebraska grew up dreaming of playing for the Cornhuskers. As a result, many players turned down scholarship offers to other universities to be a walk-on at Nebraska because that had been their destiny since birth.

However, no argument can ever be made in sports or in business that treating a certain group of people with less respect equals a recipe for success. No argument can be made to show that less competition makes a player better. And, no argument can ever be made that not rewarding your deserving players or top performers leads to victory, or is even the right thing to do.

In the end Coach Osborne had the most successful walk-on program in the country. He believed in humane respect for all players, he believed in giving walk-ons a real opportunity in the true spirit of competition, he had discipline and integrity, and he lived up to his word to give scholarships to the most deserving walk-ons who fought their way to the top of the depth chart.

In the current wake of NCAA scholarship sanctions several teams should be leaning towards following the Tom Osborne school of thought. Penn State is currently the hardest hit, losing 20 scholarships per year for four years. Only having 65 scholarship players on the roster should help put talented walk-ons in great positions to prove they can play.

On August 25, 2012, the ESPN College GameDay broadcast crew was discussing the situation at Penn State and Head Coach Bill O'Brien. Lee Corso stated what he would do; "…After the season I'd go to Nebraska. I'd see Tom Osborne. I'd find out about their walk-on program which was the best in the country, and that could help their numbers someday at Penn State. His walk-on program is going to be very, very important." Host Chris Fowler and commentators Kirk Herbstreit and Desmond Howard also talked about how impressed they were with the way Penn State Head Coach Bill O'Brien had handled the football programs situation and stated that Coach O'Brien knew how important walk-ons would be to his program. At the same time, the GameDay panel made note of how difficult it would be to recruit walk-ons against the likes of Urban Meyer (Ohio State), Brady Hoke (Michigan), Pitt, and West Virginia, among all the other schools in the Big 10 Conference.

However, I think Coach O'Brien should use this as an opportunity to pull the best walk-ons in the area to Penn State! He should discuss the realities of his new walk-on program, and they should be out recruiting and telling every potential walk-on that NOW is the best time to be a walk-on at Penn State. Since walk-ons have such a long uphill battle to play at any given university, Penn State offers them the best chance to not only play, but to play early and often. The other schools in the Big 10 don't have the scholarship problems Penn State has, and will have, for the next several years. So, if I am forced to walk-on because I don't receive a scholarship, then I am looking at Penn State to walk-on to. That is going to be the best opportunity to play.

It is my contention that the teams with the best walk-on programs are the teams playing for Conference Championships at the end of every season. They are the ones playing in Bowl games and getting lots of TV time (hence, a huge financial benefit for the athletic department).

When coaches take walk-ons seriously, great things usually happen. You can't put a stop watch on heart or determination, but you can unleash the lion within and see what happens. Coach Osborne did the right thing and it paid off. Just look at his record.

***

**Lou Holtz**
**Head Football Coach**

1969–1971 William & Mary
1972–1975 North Carolina State
1976 NY Jets
1977–1983 Arkansas
1984–1985 Minnesota
1986–1996 Notre Dame
1999–2004 South Carolina

He is considered one of the great college coaches of the modern era. Most people know that, but very few realize Lou

Holtz was a walk-on football player at Kent State in 1957 and 1958. His high school football coach took a position on the staff and encouraged Holtz to walk-on. He jumped at the chance.

Holtz did get some playing time in games but more importantly his toughness, positive attitude, commitment, and practice habits earned him great respect from his teammates.

What he learned was invaluable. He was treated like the other players and held to the same standards and accountability. As a coach this helped him in working with walk-ons because he really understood what they were going through. As a result he had several walk-ons from his teams earn playing time on Saturdays, and many were awarded scholarships, and some even went on to the NFL.

His enthusiasm was contagious when he talked about those very successful walk-ons that went through his programs. Holtz stated they are not always the most talented, the biggest, strongest, or fastest, but they did all the little things right. Coach Holtz said that if you do the little things, i.e., know your role, be patient, and work hard, you will be successful since those are the key ingredients in any field or endeavor.

When I called Coach Holtz to interview for this book his assistant told me how busy he was and I knew I would have to be patient. Weeks later I wrote Coach Holtz an email and he responded. First, he congratulated me on walking-on at USC.

Then he told me many of his walk-on players had gone on to become very successful doctors, lawyers, and business executives. Unfortunately, he also stated that due to his schedule with college football, TV spots and public appearances, he just did not have the time to accommodate me for an interview. But, he told me not to be discouraged and to keep moving forward with the project. Patience continued…

After several months passed and football season was over, I wrote him again. I told him that in true walk-on fashion I was not giving up! I felt his thoughts and opinions were vital to the book. His assistant wrote me back and said she would give the message to Coach Holtz in three days when he returned to the office. Four days later she wrote me again and said Coach would talk to me on Wednesday at noon. I was thrilled. My persistence and patience paid off.

We talked about how scholarship players and walk-ons were treated under his tutelage. He said that you can't be successful unless everyone is treated the same and everyone lives by the same core values. Core values are what hold a team together. It is when everyone holds the same core values that unity is built and respect sets in.

With regard to respect, Coach Holtz told me he would often make a point to tell his players about the sacrifice of walk-ons. He would typically do this in Spring Practice. He talked about how these walk-ons had to figure out a way to pay for school and other expenses. They sacrificed time away from their academics and the college social life. He would express his admiration for the walk-ons in front of the team so everyone would realize how invaluable they were. For without walk-ons, it would be impossible to practice the way they needed to in order to get better.

Coach Holtz talked about their sacrifice and stated that he firmly believes walk-ons should be allowed to eat free of charge after a practice has been conducted that day. He noted that many times when practice had ended, meetings were over, whirlpool treatments and showers were finished that some university cafeterias had closed. This, of course, left the walk-on to fend for himself somewhere, anywhere, except in the training table dining room where his fellow scholarship teammates were eating.

His advice to high school student athletes who do not get a scholarship, but still wish to play, is to walk-on because you love the game. He said to walk-on because you will become a better person in all areas of your life. Regardless if you get to see action on Saturdays, walk-on because you will become better prepared for life. Football teaches you about life. Coach Holtz ended our conversation by saying; "I learned more about life on the football field than I ever did in the classroom."

***

## Steve Mariucci
## Head Football Coach

| | |
|---|---|
| 1978-1979 | Northern Michigan University (RB) |
| 1980-1982 | Cal State Fullerton University (QB) |
| 1983-1984 | University of Louisville (WR) |
| 1985 | Orlando Renegades (WR) |
| 1986 | USC Football (WR/ST) |
| 1987-1989 | Cal (WR/ST) |
| 1990–1991 | Cal (OC) |
| 1992–1995 | Green Bay Packers (QB) |
| 1996 | Cal (HC) |
| 1997–2002 | San Francisco 49ers (HC) |
| 2003–2005 | Detroit Lions (HC) |

During Steve Mariucci's college coaching tenure he realized the importance of walk-ons and the vital role they played. He also realized that better quality walk-ons equaled better success for the team. The great walk-ons made the scholarship players better and vice versa. Rather than waiting for good-to-great walk-ons to come knocking on his door, he would seek them out first.

Coach Mariucci did his homework. He had long lists at every position of the top recruits not only in the nation, but also in his general area. After the high school signing day came and went he knew some players would be left out in the cold, yet exceptional players in their own right. He needed to talk to them before anyone else did so he could explain the benefits and perks of being a walk-on.

The first benefit discussed was admissions. He talked about how the athletic department could work with the admissions department to get a certain number of student athletes into the school as long as they had the minimum requirements on their GPA and SAT scores. Obviously those minimum scores would probably not be good enough for many regular students to be admitted. But, for student athletes, this could be a very huge benefit.

Additionally, Mariucci explained the athletic department had numerous tutors to assist student athletes with their studies (free of charge), not something the regular students get.

They also had state of the art weight rooms to work out in year round. Walk-ons need to work out in the weight room harder than anybody. Having access to the best of the best with strength coaches at your disposal has to be an incentive.

Lastly, having an opportunity to play college football and being part of team that will or should go to Bowl Games is an opportunity very few football players get.

***

## Terry Donahue
## UCLA Head Coach

1967 – 1970 Kansas (assistant)
1971 – 1975 UCLA (assistant)
1976 – 1995 UCLA (Head Coach)

"Opportunity is one of the most precious gifts in life." I had a wonderful discussion with longtime UCLA head coach, Terry Donahue. Not only was I honored to speak with one of the elite coaches of my generation, but I felt a sense of connection to him. You see, Terry Donahue became a Walk-On at UCLA in 1964.

Because he lived that life, the life of a walk-on, he knew what it was like which gave him the insight on how to handle walk-ons in his own football program. They got a legitimate shot to shine. Coach Donahue was, and is, all about opportunity, not only in receiving it, but in giving it to others.

For two decades he made it clear to his staff they would actively seek and recruit walk-ons and give them a real opportunity to move up. He stood by his word. "People move up with opportunity, not from a lack of opportunity."

He talked about the difficulties of being a walk-on and the rules that keep walk-ons away from training table. He too, cannot understand why the NCAA would take those opportunities away from a walk-on who is trying to improve. "It doesn't make much sense. In an age where every university is in an arms race to build multi-million dollar athletic facilities, and their coaches are earning seven figure salaries, and the walk-ons who are just trying to improve can't eat with their teammates after practice." reflected Coach Donahue.

He also hopes change is coming. In the meantime, his advice for the high school student is not to be discouraged, and to follow your dream. Getting involved in spring and summer football camps is an excellent way to elevate your skill level and get noticed by college coaches.

***

**Dabo Swinney**
**Head Coach Clemson**

| | |
|---|---|
| 1993 - 1995 | Alabama (GA) |
| 1996 - 2001 | Alabama (WR/TE) |
| 2003 - 2008 | Clemson (Asst HC/WR) |
| 2008 - Present | Clemson (Head Coach) |

Coach Dabo Swinney started his college career as a walk-on at the University of Alabama in 1990. He stated he was originally more of a crawl-on than a walk-on, but he lived in the weight room and worked on his skills as a receiver by catching balls from any quarterback who wanted to throw extra after practice. When a few receivers got hurt he got his shot. He became a three-year letterman and earned a scholarship.

After his playing days at Alabama ended he immediately became a GA, then an assistant coach. In 2003, his former wide receiver coach, Tommy Bowden, offered him an assistant position at Clemson. In 2008 he replaced Bowden as the head coach.

Today, walk-ons hold a special place in his program. As a former walk-on himself, he goes out of his way to make sure every player is treated equally. He also sticks by his rule, the best guys play. No favoritism. He said scholarship players come in all shapes and sizes and many test real well. But, once inside the lines at the collegiate level they just don't pan out. That's when you rely on your walk-ons who are stepping up and facing the challenges head-on.

***

**Gary Bernardi**
**College Football Coach**

| | | |
|---|---|---|
| 1980-86 | Arizona | O-Line, TE, WR |
| 1987-92 | USC | O-Line, TE, Special Teams |
| 1994-03 | UCLA | O-Line, TE, Recruiting |
| 2004 | No. Arizona | O-Line, Recruiting |
| 2005-09 | UNLV | O-Line, TE, Recuiting |
| 2010-12 | San Jose St. | O-Line |
| 2013 | Colorado | O-Line |

Coach Gary Bernardi has been involved with Division I college football for more than three decades. From 1980 to today, he has seen it all. I reached out to him in Colorado where he is the offensive line coach.

Walk-on's, Bernardi states, are vital to every program. You depend on walk-ons for executing plays in practice. They are critical to the overall success of programs. In the process there are always some walk-ons who stand up and stand out. They get on the game field. "You have to play your best players, period. You have to play the guys who are going to give you the best chance to win the game," he says.

Bernardi knows there are rules that are not favorable to walk-ons. But he does talk about the good opportunities for walk-ons such as getting into a school an athlete may not have gotten into on their own, and getting an opportunity to play at a major school.

Another option to consider is coming into school in January as a Grey Shirt. By Grey Shirting, you get an opportunity to participate in spring football practice, and then you can redshirt in the fall and really develop as a football player before your eligibility clock starts ticking.

***

**Don James**
**Head Coach Washington**

1956-1957 Kansas (GA)
1959-1965 Florida State (DB / DC)
1966-1967 Michigan (DC)
1968-1970 Colorado (DC)
1971-1974 Kent State (HC)
1975-1992 Washington (HC)

Coach Don James believed in the importance of a great walk-on program. He knew how successful the walk-on program was at Nebraska. Soon, he too had 150 players coming into the program in the fall. Sixty to seventy were walk-ons.

Title IX reduced his numbers of what he was allowed to have on the team. That was the only thing about Title IX he did not like. He stated the athletic programs are for the students and taking opportunity away from so many students in all sports was a mistake. He thought every sport, male or female, should have been allowed to bring in as many student athletes as they wanted. If a women's team had 300 athletes, good for them. But, the restrictions of opportunities hurt so many dreams.

Coach James told me he never understood the training table rule. "Why on earth you would make walk-ons pay for training table is just mind boggling to me. It's just a terrible rule."

He had his own personal rule that every Monday in the team meeting he would thank the scout team. He wanted his scholarship players to respect every walk-on and he wanted to remind them each week how important they were to the team.

His other rule was 'no one get's left behind.' For their bowl games, everyone traveled, including walk-ons, and everyone got all the same bowl game gifts.

The advice he would give to high school students is to have good grades. If you don't get a scholarship, you are going to need good grades to get into the school of your choice. There is only so much a coach can do even with recruited walk-ons. So, focus on your studies.

He also advised to go to football summer camps. Most big programs have summer camps and those are the times where coaches can legally talk to you, witness your ability, measure and evaluate you, and give invaluable instruction.

***

**Jackie Sherrill**
**Head Coach College Football**

| | |
|---|---|
| 1966 | Alabama (GA) |
| 1967 | Arkansas (GA) |
| 1968-1969 | Iowa State (asst.) |
| 1970-1972 | Iowa State (DC/AHC) |
| 1973-1975 | Pittsburgh (AHC) |

1976 Washington State (HC)
1977-1981 Pittsburgh (HC)
1982-1988 Texas A&M (HC)
1991-2003 Mississippi State (HC)

## 12th Man Kickoff Team

Head Coach Jackie Sherrill started the 12th Man Kickoff Team at Texas A&M in the early 1980's as a tribute to the tradition of the 12th Man, the Student Body. The history dates back to the early 1920's when a fan was pulled from the stands and told to suit up. He never got in the game, but was ready in case they needed him. Hence, the 12th Man.

Coach Sherrill's 12th Man Kickoff team was made up entirely of walk-ons and all sported the # 12 jersey (before NCAA rules disallowed more than one player to wear the same jersey number on the field at the same time).

Sherrill later wrote a book titled, "*No Experience Required*," which goes into the tradition of the 12th Man and those special walk-ons who worked harder than anyone else.

Speaking with Coach Sherrill he praised his 12 Man Team. They were always at the top of rankings for least amount of yards allowed. "Every walk-on wanted to be the guy who made the tackle; they were willing to work harder than everybody. It was a pleasure to see them in action."

***

**Rocky Seto**
**Seattle Seahawks**

1999 USC (Volunteer Asst)
2000-02 USC (GA)
2002-03 USC (S)
2004-05 USC (LB)
2006-08 USC (secondary)
2009 USC (Defensive Coordinator)
2010-Present Seattle Seahawks (Passing Game Coordinator/Defense)

Seto's story is very unique. Not too many Japanese–Americans play football, and far less walk-on at a major college and earn a scholarship. And, almost no one goes on to coach in college or at the professional level. Rocky Seto has done it all.

A die-hard fan of USC growing up in Southern California, Rocky Seto walked-on the football team under head coach, John Robinson, in 1997. A year later a new head coach, Paul Hackett, saw the talent and awarded Seto with a scholarship.

His love for the game and his desire to keep learning about football brought Seto back under Coach Hackett as a volunteer coach. He stayed on the staff as a Graduate Assistant when Pete Carroll took the reins and never looked back. He stayed on the staff until 2009 working his way up to Defensive Coordinator. When Coach Pete Carroll took the head job for the Seattle

Seahawks, Seto jumped to the professional ranks with Carroll in Seattle.

He talks about his uncommon journey and credits his faith, his unending desire to keep learning, his never give-up attitude, and making anything that stood in his way of his dream non-negotiable. “You find a way to overcome the adversity and you just don’t stop!” He said that is how he treated his walk-on situation and that is how he attacked the coaching world.

***

## Lessons For Life

Brad Budde had a storied eight-year professional football career with the Kansas City Chiefs. He was a starter on the 1978 National Champion USC Trojans and was the winner of the prestigious Lombardi Award. Budde was later inducted into the College Football Hall of Fame. Budde Founded GameDay Communications and today he speaks to groups and companies about teamwork and leadership. www.GameDayLeaders.com.

When I saw him speak I felt as though he was talking to the walk-ons of the world. It was riveting because even though he was speaking to an audience of business professionals, I could feel as though his massage was for us.

The skills a walk-on has to develop to be successful (on and off the field) are in-line, and go hand in hand with thriving in your vocation, your relationships, and in life in general. The correlation Brad speaks about is really simple; be coachable.

Being coachable means being receptive to positive influences and input. If your coach or your manager/boss is giving you advice or direction, be receptive, take it in, and heed what they are saying. Learn how to be "the one" they want to go to because they know you listen, and you get it done. They develop trust and respect in you, and of course, you get better.

Sometimes you feel no one is giving you a shot. You feel you are constantly being overlooked. Over time you develop a mental toughness that actually works to your advantage. Brad Budde calls it the "Rocky Mindset." Since you are unfamiliar with everything being handed to you, you develop a psychological resiliency of having to face difficult and demanding circumstances. That skill now becomes your advantage.

I sought Brad Budde's input for what he does and the walk-on life. He summed it up; The lowly, disrespected walk-on becomes a leader in the making fueled by passion with purpose. The daily despair becomes the stimulant to conquer their tested will through insurmountable odds forcing them to achieve their greatest potential. It is when their best is brought forth to the surface that perceptions change, respect sets in, and opportunities arise. Those are the ones who earn coveted membership in the world of leaders.

***

# Chapter 30

# Don't Ever Give Up

While this book is primarily related to football, I had to share a basketball story because it moved me so, and I think it will move you too. In fact, you may already have been moved when you saw the very first ESPY Awards on ESPN back on March 3, 1993.

Like most important dates in history when people recall where they were at that very moment, I'll bet many of you remember where you were when you heard that speech. I know I do. If you were not around back then or didn't hear it, you must go to www.JimmyV.org. Jimmy Valvano, or more affectionately called "Jimmy V" is another shining example of a walk-on!

Jimmy Valvano was a native New Yorker growing up in Queens. His older brother Nick was three-plus years his senior. In order for Jimmy to play ball with the older kids, he had to prove himself. He had to play all out all the time. The older kids were bigger, stronger, and faster, but Jimmy knew if he poured his heart and soul out on the field of battle, leaving nothing left in his tank, he would be able to participate with the older kids.

Nick Valvano never was easy on his little brother. He forced Jimmy to play harder so he could compete with the older boys. By the time Jimmy was in eighth grade his family moved 25 miles out to Seaford, NY, and he was about to play sports with kids his own age for the first time. But, Jimmy had become so good in sports that in his freshman year he was moved up to play varsity football, basketball, and baseball. Jimmy was able to play one more year with brother Nick who was a senior at Seaford High. From that point on, Jimmy V was a three-sport star earning All-County honors in all three sports.

While Jimmy excelled in all sports, and even got a lot of interest from Major League Baseball's Kansas City Athletics while in high school, he had a dream to play basketball for St. John's University, located in Queens, his boyhood stomping grounds. But, even though Jimmy was All-County in basketball, St. John's did not offer a scholarship to the 6-foot 0-inch, 155-pound Jimmy Valvano, saying he was not good enough or talented enough to earn a scholarship.

Nick Valvano believes Jimmy was just a victim of the time period. Since scouting was not like it is today, and despite being All-Everything, Jimmy did not get the big exposure he needed being out in the small Long Island town. Brokenhearted, he did not give up. Jimmy V headed to New Jersey to walk-on to the basketball program at Rutgers University. Determined to prove St. John's made a mistake and prove he was a worthy player, Jimmy

V worked his way into playing time, a scholarship, and the starting-point guard position.

Jimmy V practiced harder than anyone else because that was his nature, but also he did not want to keep borrowing money to go to college. He once joked; "I had a scholarship from the Dime Savings Bank. It took me seven years to pay it back!" In his final season, Valvano's inspiring play led his team of underdog Rutgers basketball players to the NIT Tournament where they placed third, and he was named Senior Athlete of the Year at Rutgers in 1967. Not bad for a walk-on.

Jimmy V attacked his next journey in life with the same passion and enthusiasm as he did his walk-on college career. His next goal was to be one of the best college basketball coaches around.

For 19 seasons he paced the hardwood floors and in 1983, Coach Jimmy V led his North Carolina State team to victory in the NCAA National Championship game.

Jimmy V coached until 1990, leading the Wolfpack to five more NCAA Tournaments. Unfortunately, in June 1992, Jimmy was diagnosed with bone cancer. By July, it had spread, and he was told by doctors his time was limited. ESPN held its first ESPY Awards in March 1993, and Jimmy Valvano was given the Arthur Ashe Courage and Humanitarian Award. He was helped up to the podium by his dear friend, fellow coach and broadcaster Dick

Vitale. Over the next 11 minutes Jimmy V went on to give one of the most moving speeches of all time.

He said everyone should do three things every day. “To me, there are three things we all should do every day. We should do this every day of our lives. Number one is laugh. You should laugh every day. Number two is think. You should spend some time in thought. Number three is you should have your emotions moved to tears—could be happiness or joy. But think about it. If you laugh, you think, and you cry, that's a full day. That's a heck of a day. You do that seven days a week, you're going to have something special.”

Sadly, eight weeks after his ESPY speech Jimmy V died. His tombstone reads: "Take time every day to laugh, to think, to cry." It was during his speech that he introduced the formation of The V Foundation for Cancer Research. It can be found at www.JimmyV.org. Jimmy V lived by his motto, he played by his motto, and he coached by his motto. Fittingly, the motto of The V Foundation for Cancer Research is: “Don’t Give Up…Don’t Ever Give Up!”

***

# Chapter 31
# Walk-On Secretes and Tips

Once you've landed at your collegiate destination it is time to really mentally prepare and follow a game plan. Hopefully, you are treated well and fairly, but be prepared to not receive as much love as you will witness the scholarship guys receiving. Sorry, but that's the way it is.

The scholarship players will literally be catered to right from the start. You will witness it firsthand and feel left out in the cold. People in the media department will come clamoring to setup interviews or get more information on the scholarship players. The student athlete counselors will come running down the hall to meet with every player to make sure they have all their classes lined up for the fall and have any necessary tutor's setup for ongoing help and guidance; that's not a bad thing. The university is protecting their investment and wants to make sure their student athletes are following the program so they can stay eligible. So, it is a smart move on the schools part to do all of this, but as a walk-on, just realize they won't go out of their way to do the same for you. That, most likely, will be your responsibility to investigate services you can take advantage of that are at your disposal. Also, don't be offended that you won't be first in line.

Remember, the athletic department has made a huge financial investment in the scholarship players so their needs will always come first. If there is room or time, the walk-ons will get what is left over. Just accept it since this will probably never change.

Many of the scholarship players will be treated as "mini" celebrities. You will see how people react and interact with them within the athletic building and around campus. As a walk-on, you will not receive the same adulation just because you are on the football team. In fact, once you tell someone you are on the football team you will most likely be peppered with uncomfortable questions like; "Are you on scholarship? Do you play? What number are you?"

Chances are your honest answers would be; "No, I'm a Walk-On. No, I'm on the practice squad." And, "I don't have an official number yet," or "I'm #128." All these truthful answers are a little hard to swallow especially when you see their reactions. You are no longer interesting to them. You can see it in their body language and you feel lower than dirt. So, you soon become real guarded on the information you share about yourself for fear of embarrassment. How sad it is to be a member of a Division I football program, but people actually make you feel ashamed because your moniker states you are a "walk-on." It "should" be very impressive to say you are on the football team. If that was the case, you would be feeling pretty good about yourself. But, once the questions start flying, you get chopped down pretty quickly and you just want to walk away. It can be demoralizing. With that said, let's get you focused, "walk-on style…"

## GET STARTED EARLY

Find out if you can work out at the school during the summer. Interacting with coaches and other athletes will give you a huge advantage over all the other players who report for camp in August. The coaches will know you are dedicated and you will get a good idea of where you are with regard to your strength which will help you work that much harder in the weight room. If you live too far away to participate in summer workouts, call the strength coach and ask for a workout plan for the summer you can follow on your own or with other athletes in your home town.

## SCHOOL SCHEDULE

Take the initiative and find the athletic counselors who assist the student athletes, introduce yourself and make friends with them. They are there to help all the athletes so take advantage of this and talk to them about class schedule, what services are available to you (such as tutor programs, internships, etc.), which General Education (GE) classes will or will not count towards your major, if you even know what your major will be.

I found out the hard way. I did not know what I wanted to major in for the first two years of college so I took whatever I was told to take that would keep me eligible to play football. When I decided I wanted to be a Business Major, I found out that a few of the GE courses I took during my freshman and sophomore years would not count towards a Business major and that would force me to take another semester of classes in order to graduate. I felt forced to major in Public Administration only because courses I had taken did count towards that major. I had no interest in Public Administration but I was stuck in that major because I wanted to graduate in four years.

My tip to you; know thy major. And if you don't have one picked out, strongly consider a Business Major from the start so you take the right courses. When you are through playing football and graduate, you will most likely go out into the business world so you might as well have a Business Major in your back pocket.

## BE HONEST

Are you really good enough to play on Saturday? Here is THE most important question that you have to answer honestly. You have to look in the mirror and be as truthful as you can possibly be. Can I outwork the scholarship players in front of me on the depth chart at my position and compete for a travel roster spot and a place on special teams?

You may not know the true answer at the very beginning of your freshman year when you are getting the pads on and hitting with the big boys for the first time in August or September. It might take some time for you to evaluate yourself against the other incoming freshmen and older players. But, in short order, knowing you will get stronger and faster as time goes on, you should be able to evaluate yourself and ask the question, "Do I have the talent to play on Saturday?"

This is extremely important in my opinion because you can literally place yourself in one of two categories. A "Practice Squad Walk-On" or a "Game Day Walk-On." If you are totally content with being a practice player and know you will probably never get to see the Game Day field, then bless you. I admire your commitment to dedicate your time, effort and body to the team and the program, basically free of charge. That is extremely admirable. I applaud you!

However, if you are a Game Day Capable Walk-On and playing on Saturday is your only option, then you have a slightly different road to travel than your counterpart Practice Walk-On.

For me, I realized immediately two major things in my first few days of practice. As far as talent was concerned, I felt that I could play at the Division I level. However, I also realized that I was grossly undersized and not nearly as strong as I needed to be in order to be effective. I was a tailback in high school and on day one of my freshman year I was moved to fullback. The difference between the weight of our starting tailback and our starting fullback was 60 pounds! I had the body size of a tailback and was asked to be scout team fullback against one of the best defenses in the country! I realized that as a 195 lb. freshman I was at least 30 to 40 lbs lighter than I should have been. There was only one solution; live in the weight room.

## STRENGTH / NUTRITION

Here is my big tip aside from living in the weight room. You need to work out during the hours when there are fewer scholarship guys working out. That means get there when the strength coach opens the doors in the morning. That might be 5 or 6 a.m. Suck it up and DO IT! Here are the major advantages. First, very few people will take the initiative to get out of bed and drag themselves to the gym at the crack of dawn. Secondly, since fewer will be in the gym, you have the strength coach's personal attention. He will watch and correct your form and help you. You will basically get one-on-one training from one of the best strength coaches in the country. Regardless of which school you attend, especially if it is a Division I School, those strength coaches are very good at what they do and they are devoted to those that are passionate about working out! Strength coaches love to coach. The weight room is their domain and if you are dedicated to what they love, they will help you. Just by getting there in the morning and showing your commitment will motivate them to help you achieve your goals. And when they report to the head coach at the end of the day on who worked out, your name will be the first that is mentioned.

I am determined to overturn the NCAA training table rule so all walk-on student athletes in all sports get the proper nutrition they need and deserve. Until then, study your nutritional facts. Look up which foods are best for your recovery, when and what you should eat before and after you work out. What snacks will work for you and which ones will set you back. Remember, you need every advantage you can get to excel at your peek state. Nutrition is vital to your development as an athlete.

## TRAINING ROOM

The training staff has many responsibilities, none of which are to cater to the walk-ons who have a hang-nail or a bruised pinky finger. They will, of course, help you if you come knocking on their door; but, be very careful on how much time you spend in the training room. You never want to be labeled as one of "those guys" who loves to lie on a medical table with a bag of ice and take up space; let the scholarship guys do that. Get your bag of ice and lay on your couch at home. You are going to get dinged up with bumps and bruises all over your body. You just have to know the difference between being really sore and having an injury. Yes, if you have an injury, by all means, seek help. But, if you are just looking for a student trainer to give you a massage on your aching body, then go elsewhere.

The trainers give a full report to the head coach on every player who came into their room and the treatment they received. This is not a list you want your name on if you are a walk-on. If the coach thinks you are too dinged up to practice 100% you may be pulled out of a drill or out of a scrimmage. As a walk-on, you need those reps and opportunities to shine. Remember, practice is YOUR game day. Please note I am not suggesting you play through an injury; but, you must play through discomfort and pain.

I made friends with all the members of the staff from the head trainer, to his assistants, and to the student trainers. When I felt something was a little wrong with my shoulder, I went to the student trainers first. My hope was that nothing was seriously wrong and I could play through my discomfort. If the remedy was ice, then I would just take a bag home with me. I did not want to get on the Trainers Injury List; I had a game the next day. Be smart about your body and your time. If you are not seriously injured, get in and out of the training room quickly. Hypochondriac is not a word you want associated with you as a walk-on. Let the scholarship guys hang out in the training room so they get taken out of drills and scrimmages in practice. That's when your name will be called to step in and step up!

## PLAYBOOK

I know college is filled with fun, fun, fun and you want to hit every party on Fraternity and Sorority Row. That might be doable and fit in your schedule; *but* if you are serious about being a Game-Day Walk-On, you better take care of two things before the parties. Get your school work done and know your playbook inside and out.

A walk-on's chance to play on Saturday is slim. The opportunities in practice are few and far between to prove you are Game Day capable. So, when the opportunity presents itself, you MUST take advantage of it. This is your time to stand out. There is no faster way back to the bench than not knowing your playbook. Your assignments are vital on every play. Every play, regardless of your position, has equal value on all eleven players. The ball may be going to the other side of the field, but what you are doing on your side is critical to the overall success of the play. You cannot "ease up" when the play is going away from you. That will set a pattern for the opposition to read how you act or react when the ball is not on your side. That could set the stage for disaster later in the game.

Because scholarship players are treated like kings, most think they will get endless opportunities. That's mostly true, but when they don't know their assignments in practice, the coach may scream for you to get in the scrimmage and show how it is done. This is YOUR time, YOUR shot, YOUR opportunity. Make the most of it by knowing your playbook!

## TECHNIQUE

At the college level your technique needs to improve tenfold from high school. The game is bigger, stronger, faster and smarter. You need the very best technique not only to survive, but to be effective. You will learn these new skills at the next level, but you cannot rely only on your personal repetitions to absorb this knowledge. You must watch the upperclassmen in front of you and really pay close attention to the coach as he corrects the other guys. You need to learn from other players' mistakes while waiting your turn in line. If you visualize doing the assignment based on how the coach has instructed, you can get visual reps in your head before your turn is even up. Pay attention on every play on what the coach is teaching. You can learn every play even when you are not in the drill or scrimmage. Your technique can improve by watching, observing, visualizing, and when it is your turn, by doing it! Stay focused!

## LEVERAGE

In my humble opinion leverage is the number one most critical factor in all of football. As a walk-on in 1988 I was placed on scout team offensive. As a fullback I had to play against one of the nation's top defenses. My main target was Junior Seau. I was not stronger, faster, quicker, or more talented than Seau, that is for sure; but, I ultimately ended up having good success against him in practice. How? Since I knew I could not out muscle him head-to-head I had to come up with a strategy to contain him. I figured this all out through hundreds of reps against Junior and the other monster beasts on defense. If I could put myself in a position to have better "leverage" than my opponent, then I stood a much better chance at accomplishing my task.

From my fullback position, if I had to block Seau who was playing outside linebacker, I wanted help from my offensive tackle. I would run at Seau at a slightly wider angle so it basically forced him to go inside of me. If I could get him to go inside of me, I could immediately change course and crash down on him and try like hell to knock him into the tackle and sandwich him. If I disrupted his advancement for just a split second, I was successful because the tailback would be running off my outside hip or the pass would have been thrown by the time Seau got to the QB. I did not have to knock him down, I just had to knock him off balance or seal him away just long enough for the tailback to race by.

Getting low was also critical to my success. They say “low pads wins.” Well, that is true most of the time, but not all of the time. If you get too low you wind up face first in the turf. But, if you are low enough where you are still under control of your body, then you can make some great blocks and move the linebacker just enough to make it a successful play. It’s a game of inches, but not just for first-downs. If you move a defender just out of reach of a hand grab on the jersey as the ball carrier races by, you will have a big play.

One of my biggest pet peeves was our “ISO” play. ISO stands for isolation. It is the fullback against the linebacker, mano-a-mano, straight forward, full blast from eight yards apart sprinting at each other for the kill. This is the dumbest play in all of football. At this level, where you have two very aggressive football players going all out, there is reason for concern. These collisions are probably the worst in football. You want to investigate head trauma? Start with the guys who are engaged in ISO hits. They are brutal and scary to watch. In the tight squeeze between the linemen, there is not a lot of room to put your head off to the side and hit with your shoulder pads. The massive hit usually takes place helmet to helmet. There is pretty much no other way. Bells are rung, vision is blurry, the pain intense. It's an ugly scene.

I did not want to deal with that on a regular basis. So, I used another technique to get my leverage. I used vision.

## VISION

I learned to place a block before I even got to where I was going by using my vision. It was not taught to me by the running back coach. He was at the other end of the field with the starting offense. I was on my own to teach myself. It was a game of survival for me. Realizing the defense keyed off of where I was looking, I used my eyeballs to fake my direction. I would literally look to the outside of the tackle even though my assignment was straight up the middle for a terrifying ISO block. By doing so, the linebacker would key in on my eyeballs and assume I was looking to go outside the tackle. At the snap of the ball I would take one hard step like I was going right off tackle and be looking there as well. On my second step I immediately changed direction straight up field. If I could get the linebacker to "bite" on my phony vision and my fake first step, I put him one step out of position. In the middle of his second step he would have to change direction from heading off tackle to straight up the middle to meet me.

The first mission was accomplished. I would now engage with the middle linebacker at a tiny angle rather than a straight on, head to head collision. At my tiny angle I could inflict the blow of my block with my shoulder pad, rather than my helmet. That was much safer and felt so much better. Also, I could create a seal just big enough for the running back to make a cut away from the LB as I sealed him off with my helmet.

I used vision to get leverage. I used leverage to set the stage for my technique. I used my technique to create a seal or separation through my block. And that usually gave us the time for the tailback to run by or the quarterback to throw. When I did that, I won the battle of that play. Huddle up. Let's do it again.

## THE MENTAL GAME

There will be times when you don't feel you are getting a fair shot. You will be frustrated and your stomach will be turning. You will be playing a guessing game with yourself and the coaches. Will the coach put me in the scrimmage today? Will he give me a fair shot to prove myself worthy? Are all the scholarship guys going to play 99% of the scrimmage in practice and I will get two garbage time plays to end the day?

Again, a major investment has been made in the scholarship players and they are determined to have those players play and prove the coach made a great decision when he gave that player a scholarship. Also, remember that these coaches typically spend years recruiting and watching hundreds of hours of film on these prospective scholarship players. They spend hundreds of thousands of dollars to fly all over the country going to their homes to speak with their parents. They plead with the mothers and fathers to encourage their sons to attend their universities enabling them the opportunity to play and succeed. They tell the parents they will take care of their son and they make all kinds of promises to the young man and his family. Do you think a coach is going to easily let some no-name walk-on come in out of nowhere and take over? Not a chance. Hence, the mental game.

I was not prepared for this mental game my true freshman year. When I played really well there was no one there to pat me on the back. When I thought I had proven myself to move up the depth chart, there was no such luck. When I outplayed my competition I felt like I was on a deserted island. Thankfully, starting in my second season, I did have an outside source, my mentor Jim Walsh, to call and talk to during those trying times.

My suggestion is to have someone you can talk to when times get tough. It might be your parents or other family members. It might be your high school coach. But, having someone you can talk to helps, just to get it off your chest. For me, I did not want to tell my parents or brothers how sad I was because I did not want them to feel my pain too. They knew I was mad because I was not getting the opportunities I felt I deserved, but they did not know how incredibly down I was and that I had shut off friends and spent a lot of time alone because I had no desire to go out and have fun. It was a tough time for me due to my lack of mental readiness.

Talking to my mentor lifted my spirits and gave me hope and encouragement to stay the course and remain focused on my ultimate goal of playing on Saturday. Over time things started to happen for me; I believe they will for you too.

## DISCIPLINE

Even though you are not a star as a walk-on, you are still associated with the team. You may not get press if you do something good on the field, but they will print your name for all to see if you do something bad or illegal off the field. With that said, anything you do that is negative in person or on social media will be jumped on by the press. If there is a big party and the police are called and you are there, you better walk the other way. If there is a fight, if there is someone cheating in school, if someone does something illegal and you are even remotely nearby or associated with the incident, you are gone from the team in the blink of an eye. You are expendable. The university and the athletic department go through great pains to run a clean and efficient program. Anyone not walking the straight and narrow will be dealt with quickly. Scholarship players caught in the middle of mischief "might" receive some form of punishment and be given a second chance. But, if a walk-on is involved in anything unbecoming of team standards, he's gone. The athletic department will distance themselves from a walk-on in a heartbeat if he has done something wrong. Every year student athletes find trouble and every year players are dismissed from the team because they are not mature enough to do the right thing. Let the scholarship players get busted for bad behavior. That gives you another opportunity to show what you can do in practice.

This piece of advice may be the least popular among the high school students, but perhaps the most popular with their parents. Don't ruin your upward mobility potential with piercings and body art. I know young adults think it is cool and all the rage. But, you don't run the show. Coaches and your future employers do. I know you don't understand or agree with this at 18, but here is the reality. Many adults in position of power may not like body piercings and tattoos. If they see that on you, you become labeled. And if they are not a big fan of your body art, you may have lost a huge opportunity and you will never know it.

Here is a true story for you. A Division I coach I interviewed for this book was super high on a walk-on. A scholarship was available and the head coach walked into the locker room to tell the young man to report to his office so he could deliver the great news. When he walked into the locker room, he found the shirtless young man sporting two nipple rings.

The coach told him to take them out and never to put them back in. The coach was so disgusted he waited until the following semester before he awarded the walk-on with the scholarship. Because of nipple rings that walk-ons' parents had to foot the bill for tuition for another semester.

You may think that is ridiculous, but that is life. Think about your future employment. What if your tattoo is visible with business casual clothes on? What if your future boss does not want to see your tattoo nor have it be seen by their clients? You may not get a job because of it. You may not be promoted because of it. Body ink and piercings may be totally hip and cool in your late teens and early twenty's. But one day it could cost you a lot of money and a great job and you will probably never be told that was the reason you did not get the gig. Please be smart.

Keep your priorities in order. Take advantage of the counselors to get the classes you need and the help you can get. Be honest of where you are in relation to the other players. Know your playbook inside and out. Learn the skills and techniques the coaches teach to others by paying close attention to get your visual reps in. Using vision and leverage can compensate for just about anything. If you stay disciplined, use your knowledge, know your plays, and work your tail off in the weight room, I think I will see you on Saturday afternoon.

***

# Chapter 32

# Graduating Walk-On

When graduation comes around, when his time in the walk-on world is up, you can rest assure he learned more than he ever thought possible. He was thrown into a world very few people get to experience. Some of it was very painful. Yet, he survived. Along the way he experienced every emotion humanly possible and had to endure most of it by himself.

Before he died, Coach Jimmy V said in his speech at the 1993 ESPY awards that "If you can laugh, think, and cry every day, that's something special. That is a full day."

Every graduating walk-on has had a lot of full days. That emotional experience is probably more than any other student has had in their life. The emotional rollercoaster may last between one and five years. That tenure can be a full-life experience in, and of, itself.

When it is all over, you won't get an award for being a walk-on. You won't be part of a parade or attend a dinner with a funny roast. You won't put on a cap and gown and walk across a stage to thunderous applause to receive a degree for majoring in Walk-On Psychology from Walk-On U (although you probably should). In fact, most people won't even recognize you for what you just experienced, learned, and achieved. Sure, you will get a few pats on the back from family and friends but they won't have a clue to what you have truly been through and accomplished. They might have heard some of your stories along your journey, but they did not 'walk-on' in your shoes and will never truly know what it was really like to be you.

Walk-Ons experience the UGLY: discrimination, bias, favoritism, prejudice, unfairness, fear, hatred, humiliation, disbelief, doubt, distrust, physical pain, emotional pain, animosity, bitterness, resentment and politics.

Walk-Ons experience the BAD: hostility, anger, indignation, broken promises, annoyance, fury, ire, wrath, sadness, stress, heartbreak, worry, second guessing, confusion, uncertainty, incomprehension, shame, and embarrassment.

Walk-Ons experience the GOOD: accomplishment, hope, optimism, confidence, courage, possibilities, determination, strength, grit, diligence, tenacity, resolve, leverage, patience, persistence, tolerance, fortitude, perseverance, character building, loyalty, devotion, teamwork, and brotherhood.

There is a lot of emotion in all those feelings, and walk-ons feel it. When the pit is stuck in your throat, or your stomach is tied up in knots, those are heavy emotions to deal with. When you want to quit you won't because you want to keep going to see that light. It is the fire in your belly that forces you to stay the course, searching for the light you believe is somewhere off in the distance. You can't see it yet, but its close enough you can feel it.

The walk-on emotions will take you to the gates of hell. If you are fortunate, you will ascend and come back to earth. Soon, your emotional journey may take you to some heavenly places you thought you might never see. When you get there, the enjoyment will be that much sweeter. For you were furthest away from this joy. You had the longest road to travel. Your journey reached great lengths to rip everything from your heart. A whirlwind of emotions swept over you and your solo journey was on-the-job training.

Your survival was due to that special something that dwells within you that few people have. Some say that people who do extraordinary things have the "it" factor. Actually, you have the "Walk-On" factor.

Walk-ons are faced with rejection early and often. Some quit the team almost immediately. Those who have the "Walk-On" factor hold steady, stay the course, work hard, hope, and pray that things will slowly get better. Sometimes they do and sometimes they don't. A great majority of the time walk-ons do not get to play on a regular basis, if it all; and their sheer passion to bust their tails day in and day out is a long and often discouraging journey. It's even worse when scholarship players ask the walk-ons why they are even out there. Many admit that if they did not have a scholarship they sure as heck would not be out there practicing as a walk-on, but it is in those worst of times you unknowingly are becoming better in so many things.

Walk-ons receive tons of advice from scores of people. They send your mind in a million different directions. Ultimately, you follow your heart and do what your gut tells you. When you guess wrong, you learn from it. You spend a lot of time thinking, but, in the end you carry with you a resumė of experiences unparalleled to most.

When you enter the working world you will be much further advanced than many of your fellow graduates. When adversity hits "regular" recent graduates, they are often dealing with these strenuous issues for the first time in their life. However, for the walk-on, that adversity road has been traveled before, many, many times. The walk-on will not be shocked or dumbfounded. There'll be no "deer in headlights" look when these tough situations strike. The walk-on will keep calm and carry on. The thinking cap of how to handle that adversity will be in full force and solutions and ideas will be forthcoming.

As it is with most people the walk-on will be engrossed in relationships with family, friends, a spouse, and children. Like all relationships there will be challenges, tough decisions, and household discussions. There is no question that I am a better man and father today because of my walk-on experiences.

Very few people in this world are walk-ons. Approximately 250,000 high school seniors are playing football in America each year. From that number, approximately 4,500 will get scholarships to play Division I Football in both FBS (I-A) and FCS (I-AA) or 0.018%, and out of those 250,000 high school football players, about 2,500 will walk-on to a Division I program, or 0.01%. Only about 0.002% or 500 walk-ons will be playing on Saturday in all of Division I. To take it one step further, just 100 walk-ons will be playing in Division I Bowl Games in December and January every year which equates to just 0.0004% of the United States high school football population. Now that is a special group!

Your priceless experiences, which can be extremely difficult for an 18, 19, or 20 year old to handle and endure, will get you ready for life. You won't realize it at the time, but you're getting an A+ in the education of a lifetime. It sets the tone early and prepares you for the working world, your relationships, being a parent, and the treasures of friendships. When you take those same skills you learned out there on the field and transfer them into your daily life you have a leg up on just about everybody. I look back at the true value of my USC experience; the ugly, the bad, the not so bad, the good and the great. As hard as it was at times and as much as it pushed me to the limit, I am grateful for my experience. I'm pleased with my accomplishments and I am honored and damn proud to be a Trojan!

The beautiful thing about being a walk-on is that it is such an extremely small, coveted group with a unique experience for membership. The journey requires a relentless, no-quit attitude and a mental toughness that bends, but does not break. These traits are not coachable. They are innate.

The letters "W.O." in Walk-On are no longer a shameful, scarlet letter I once loathed. Today, I wear those letters proudly across my chest like a silver star or a purple heart. Yes, I may have earned a scholarship, but I respect the walk-on journey so much that I'd rather keep that title and be known as one for life.

Those who walked-on yesterday know exactly what I am talking about. Those walk-ons engaged in the fight today are in the middle of an uncommon world. And those who will become a walk-on tomorrow will also be part of a special passage that will change your life. But, all will look back one day, cherish, treasure, and appreciate being part of Walk-On U.

When you become a member of Walk-On U, you will endure ugly things, bad things and good things. I have talked about all three in this book.

As for the ugly and the bad, those feelings will go away in time. You will eventually shed the fresh memories of painful tears and look back and realize it was a powerful experience.

But for the good, people who will be talking to you throughout your life, asking what it was like, thinking it is so cool you played way back when at a Division I program. They will befriend you because you ran through that tunnel that 99.99% of young men only dream about, but never get to experience. You will meet people in the work place and develop an instant rapport. It will open doors, grant you meetings and close deals. Every party or special event will bring new people wanting to know what it was like being you during those times. While you once felt so distant when you were knee deep in the walk-on experience, you are now propelled to the forefront of conversations with people wanting to meet you. The beauty of being a coveted member of ***Walk-On U*** is that in the end, the "good" never ends!

***

# Chapter 33
# Today – Where and Why

The 1991 year, my last, had me as second team fullback. However, early in the season our offensive coaching staff put in a Power I formation, utilizing two fullbacks in the game at the same time. As a result I received a ton of playing time, even starting some games when we opened up with the Power I formation.

If you grew up in the 1970's and 1980's, you grew up watching the iconic Pittsburg Steelers and one of the greatest wide receivers of all time, Lynn Swann. You also grew up listening to one of the most recognizable voices in all of sports, announcer Al Michaels.

Lynn Swann might best be known for his four Super Bowl victories and the Super Bowl X MVP Award. Al Michaels might best be known for announcing one of the greatest sports moments in history, the 1980 USA Olympic Hockey team, when they beat the heavily favored Russians. While the seconds ticked down to zero, Al Michaels exalted, *"Do you believe in miracles? YES!"*

About a decade later, Swann and Michaels teamed up to do play-by-play announcing for college football with ABC Sports. One Saturday afternoon I was running at fullback all day as our first team fullback was a little dinged up. Our wide receiver,

Curtis Conway, was also playing some quarterback. Curtis (a 12 year NFL veteran) liked to run more than throw. On one play, I was in the backfield by myself. Conway took to the snap, rolled out to his left and ran. I was in front of him and ran too. Curtis ran a 4.3 forty. I ran a four day 40. But I digress… I took off after the linebacker closing in on Curtis and chop-blocked him to the ground allowing Curtis to get outside and gain more yards.

My parents taped the game on their VCR and the next time I was home I watched it. Al Michaels and Lynn Swann were the announcers of that game. You could hear Michaels saying; "…Conway's in at quarterback. Lavin's his fullback. He drops back; he's rolling left, now he's going to run the ball. He gets a block from Lavin and eventually goes out of bounds." They showed a replay in slow-motion and Lynn Swann jumped in, "…[Conway] he's not going to win an Academy Award for the fake pass, but look at that great block by number 39, Tim Lavin is his name."

When I heard them talking about me I got chills. It may have been weeks later when I watched the game, but I have to admit it added to my highlights of the season. I thought that was pretty cool.

After my playing days as a Trojan were over, I kept knocking on doors. I received a tryout with the San Francisco 49ers and then went on to play a season in Australia for the

Brisbane Bulldogs. When I came back to the States I got another tryout with the Oakland Raiders, but ultimately my dream of playing in the NFL was not realized.

When the dust settled and my career was spent I experienced a period of time where I could not watch football on TV or even attend games as a spectator which lasted a solid five years. I was sad it was over after playing the game every autumn dating back to the age of seven. I did not want to break up with the game, but the game was ready to break up with me. Time had run its course and my clock showed 0:00.

Stepping away was hard and it was easier not to be reminded I was not in uniform by being glued to the TV on those fall Saturday and Sunday afternoons. Melancholy set in because of my deep rooted association. It was tough to say goodbye before I was ready. But, I had to go on.

The entire experience had meaning. I toiled with the ups and downs of the whole package and tried to bury the ugly while reliving the good. The ugly parts of being a walk-on had a firm grip on me, another reason I had to turn away from watching games on TV for so many years.

However, time and distance made me stronger and I realized I was using the same skills in the working world. The skills I once used on the field, especially the mental part, were leading the charge of my life. In the late 1990's I started my own business in the promotional products industry and had to call it none other than; *Mad Dog Promos*.

By 1999 my business took off and was gaining steam monthly. My first clients were Hewlett-Packard, PeopleSoft, and Sun Microsystems. Because of them, every new startup in the Silicon Valley wanted to order premiums from me. It was the "dot com" era and orders were pouring in at an unbelievable rate. I was preparing to buy my first house. I was shopping for that mansion on the hill. I had the down payment ready to go. And almost overnight the dot com world went bust.

Not only did the orders come to a screeching halt, but the companies that I had extended credit to went belly up, never paying their bills. I lost everything and was left with a mountain of debt. Devastated, I had to lean on skills I learned as a walk-on. It was all I had. The money was gone, but not my desire. I was able to control the knots in my stomach because I had done it so many times before, years earlier.

Weathering the economic storm I was able to keep Mad Dog Promos open on a shoestring budget and creative partnerships. The company is still alive and kicking today.

I experienced some tough times at USC during my tenure. Nevertheless, those times were vital in my development as a person. The Trojan spirit engulfed me and I feel more connected to the USC family today than I did when I was a student athlete.

When I moved back to Southern California in 2005, the Trojan Football Alumni Club (TFAC) reached out to me. I met with them at a board meeting, joining former Trojan players spanning over five decades. I was reunited with brothers I never met, but to whom I felt a connection. Within a few months I was on the executive board and after just two years I was unanimously elected President of TFAC.

I came full circle. I know where my heart is. I'm a Trojan and I bleed Cardinal and Gold.

**What's Next:**

Despite walk-ons across the country defying the odds every year, this is not the best we can do. The treatment and rules need to change.

If you were to ask any leader of any organization if they reached their peak, they would say emphatically, NO! There is always room for improvement. No good leader, CEO, head coach, or owner would ever say, "We have the best people working for us and we just can't grow, or get better. We have reached the top and there is nothing else we can do." That would never happen.

Every year the NCAA makes scores of changes to policies and rules in college sports dictating what student-athletes can and cannot do. NCAA President Mark Emmert has promised sweeping changes within the NCAA organization to make it better. We must not leave out the forgotten walk-on with these changes.

The time has come for someone to stand up for walk-ons. Now is the time for change. We are not asking for cash, tuition, books or room and board. But if walk-ons are going to play in any Division I program, they need the same tools to improve and maintain their health and safety. They need to be protected and treated with respect.

**Training-Table:** Walk-ons should be granted a seat at training-table when their sport is providing it during the year, effective immediately. This goes for all sports, male and female.

**Transferring:** Since walk-ons receive no funding from the athletic department, and the NCAA does not even ask for their progress report in the classroom, there should be no reason why a walk-on, who is not receiving any playing time, should have to sit out a year if he decides to transfer. If a walk-on is on the rise, but the coach just won't give him an opportunity to play or provide him with a scholarship that by all accounts he feels he has truly earned, why handcuff him? Apparently, he is not good enough and no one cares about him. So why penalize the walk-on for seeking a better opportunity elsewhere? Walk-ons should have the freedom to move on if they're not allowed to move up.

**Health Insurance:** Every institution should cover the health insurance of a walk-on who has made the team. Trying out is one thing. But once that player has proven himself and has dedicated his life to the team, then that institution should be obligated to pay for the insurance of the young student athlete who has committed himself or herself to their program.

**Protection.** Coaches need to be educated on helmet collisions and how it affects the brain. By understanding more about head trauma and how the damaged is caused, we may have fewer concussions. And we may eliminate some vicious practice drills, usually with walk-ons in the middle of them getting their heads slammed to the turf, in favor of less life altering impacts.

**Respect:** When a walk-on is officially part of the team, and the team receives awards and gifts for Bowl games or other special events, the walk-on should receive the same swag as the scholarship players, including rings, watches, apparel, and other accessories. When the team travels to a non-conference game, and the rule allows everyone to travel, then everyone should travel including the walk-ons.

I understand every one of these rule changes or adjustments would have to be revised with parameters to prevent situations from getting out of control. I am volunteering myself to the NCAA to represent the unrepresented walk-ons at the table. I am open to being the first voice of the Walk-On Commission. We need a seat at the table. I want to step up and step in.

Remember, as I stated, giving up is not in our DNA, so I will forever stand up for the walk-ons and be their spokesman for change. We cannot look at the current situation and say, “Yes, this is the best we can do!” Because, no, it is not the best we can do.

Coaches may not build their team around a walk-on, but upon a walk-on’s back they build their team.

* * *

# AFTERWORD

## Talk to Me!

## Help Us, Help Them

The very purpose of this book was not only to shed the reality light on the world of walk-ons, but to help set a better stage for the walk-ons of tomorrow. We can do this by sharing your stories of how YOU overcame adversity in your walk-on battle. I want to hear from all of you, both male and female, and in all sports. It does not have to be just football.

So many of you have inspiring, uplifting stories from softball, baseball, basketball, golf, tennis, volleyball, etc., that I want to share them with the world. I want the sequel to this book in the ongoing ***Walk-On U*** series to tell YOUR story of struggle, pain, determination, and success. I want to print your stories from yesteryear so we can help inspire our walk-on brothers and sisters of tomorrow. Your stories will be posted on the website and we will print as many stories as we can in the next book.

Although this first volume was almost entirely centered around football, ***Walk-On U*** is really a Fraternity and Sorority combo-association comprised of a special breed of individuals whose passion to play the game and prove all others wrong trumps all the negative experiences and private hell one may be forced to endure. Members of ***Walk-On U*** instinctively know that abandoning your personal dream and bailing out on your inner strength is just not an option because times get tough and even miserable.

Tell me your story of how you took these life-learning principals and applied them in your life after college. Share with us how being a walk-on shaped your destiny in your personal life and in your vocation. By sharing our stories in all sports, male and female, we can help the next wave of walk-ons better prepare for the uncommon journey they are about to endure.

Let's also build our ***Walk-On U*** membership database of former ***Walk-Ons*** and ***Fans of Walk-Ons*** who are full supporters of these inspiring underdogs. Click on the MEMBERSHIP tab at www.Walk-OnU.com and fill out your information. We will be able to keep you posted on future Walk-On U special events.

For those wishing to give comment, I welcome your feedback. Please email me directly from the Contact Us tab on the website, or you can visit our Facebook or Twitter pages also found at: www.Walk-OnU.com

We need to band together as fans nationwide, heck, worldwide, and guide the NCAA member institutions to rewrite, amend or eliminate altogether the unfair and outdated rules that keep walk-ons down. There needs to be updating regarding training table, insurance, and transferring. Stand up with me! Go to the Walk-OnU.com website for more information and help us change the walk-on rules for the better. Together we can lead the way for righteous change.

Finally, Thank You! Thank you for taking the time to read a seldom talked about culture of uncommon individuals who are not necessarily looking for fame, just a little respect and opportunity. They are a unique group willing to do whatever it takes, physically, mentally, and emotionally, to prove they are worthy to rise up while the "**SYSTEM**" is pushing them down. Thank you for allowing me to share my story. My reflections brought me back in time and it often moved me to tears which only inspired me even more to get this book done so I could share with sports fans and help the next generation of walk-ons have a better future.

Follow your heart, and then make it happen!

- Tim Lavin

***

# Acknowledgments

To my beautiful wife Suzanne, and our three-year-old daughter Leah, thank you for your love, support and patience. It means the world to me, and I love you so much it hurts. The past several years, and especially the past few months, I have locked myself in our office writing, rewriting, and editing. I was not as attentive as I should have been, which made this whole book-writing process that much harder. Suzanne, thank you for your understanding, and I promise to take you shopping—right after football season. Leah, we're going to the park!

I dedicated this book to my parents, Ed and Derreth Lavin, because their unyielding support of me and my two brothers for over 40-plus years is the greatest gift any child could ever ask for—period! My parents supported us playing sports year round for three decades. They came to every game from T-Ball and Pop Warner through high school and beyond. They stood by me in my darkest hours with 100 percent conviction so I could press on in search of my football dreams. My parents are my rock, and I love and thank them for everything they have given me since day one.

Next, I salute and thank my brothers, Jay and Terry, for being my biggest fans. For years they kicked my butt up and down the playgrounds. Now that I think about it, that was my first experience of being a walk-on! I walked on the field at the park or in the backyard expecting to play with the big boys. I always got to play, but they made me pay for it in between the street lights.

Jay actually took the photo of me that would ultimately become the cover of this book on the day of the Rose Bowl game against Michigan on January 1, 1990. Terry, a writer in his own right, got involved in my editing process and contributed greatly. Thank you Jay and Terry for being there and rooting for me. Love you guys.

To Jay's wife, my sister-in-law Mary, and their three beautiful girls, Kaleigh, Julia and Sarah, I miss you and love you so much.

To all the girls Terry has dated, so nice to meet you.

To my in-laws, Phil and Carolyn Thoreson, thank you for all your love, help, and support. The endless hours of watching our toddler is exhausting, we know, and you did it with a smile, even though sometimes it was a forced smile. I can't thank you enough. You're a godsend. And a big thank-you to Carolyn's mother, affectionately known as Grammy, who will turn 99 years old in October 2013, and who encouraged me to "hurry up" and finish the book. Love you Grammy.

To my brother-in-law Jeff (Suzanne's brother) and my sister-in-law Lynnette, as well as their two children Ryan and Kate, thank you for your love and support, especially in looking after little Leah.

To the extended family and relatives on both sides of the Lavin and Thoreson clans, thank you for all your love and support!

I was truly blessed to have Jim Walsh guide me through my walk-on odyssey. He had a tremendous impact on my life, and I will forever be grateful. Jim, when I was at my lowest, you picked me up mentally and physically. When I was in pain and pondering my next move, you made me feel like I won the Heisman Trophy. You gave me strength to carry on when I was not sure if I could. You were with me during the long, hot summer days helping me to run faster and preparing my mind for the walk-on journey. You were with me on the phone for hours in the fall when I was wondering why my world was upside down. You were with me even when you weren't there physically during my training sessions as I pictured you standing near, encouraging me to lift the weights one more rep, or run just one more 40.

I was a walk-on when I met and started working with you. I earned a football scholarship after working with you for just one year. Thank you, Jim Walsh, for being there for me and with me at the most crucial time in my life.

To Chaminade College Preparatory, *THANK YOU* for providing me the best education that is available on the west coast. May I also take this opportunity to thank every teacher I ever had, especially at Chaminade. And let me publically apologize to every teacher I slightly annoyed with my sometimes not-so-perfect behavior. I mean it.

To Pete Elliot, who believed in the project, met with me several times to discuss the material, organized the editing team, arranged our meetings, made invaluable suggestions, and gave opinions on the content and the chapter sequence, I say thank you.

Over the summer, I was very fortunate to acquire a team of interns to help build and add content to the Walk-OnU.com website. I have to thank Anthony Aschieris, Amanda Althoff, Sean Robb, Jon-Thomas Royston, and Daniel Maroko. You rock!

Thank you to my social media guru, Scott Capone of Capone Strategies, www.caponestrategies.com, for getting "Walk-On U" in the social media game.

To my incredible friends and close associates who gave me legal advice, book opinions, suggestions, guidance, financial recommendations and assistance, all to keep "Walk-On U" moving forward, I thank you so very much. Special thanks to Tommy Dexter, Ray and Shannon Campuzano, Rob Wiley, John Phalen, Erik Colandone, Tom Bacon, Steve Fortunato, Shane Foley, Brad

Leggett, my Chaminade Cronies (Jimbo Strong*), and the Trojan Football Alumni Club.

* = Lt. James (Jimmy, Jimbo) Farrell. Duty, Honor, Courage, Inspiration, Leader, Lieutenant, Husband, Father, and Friend. A True Friend.

My fellow walk-on fraternity and sorority brothers and sisters, both known and unknown, all across the nation; we did it. We know the real deal and now is the time we band together to share it with others. Some of you who shared with me your heartfelt stories of your journey, please understand that space was the enemy—I just couldn't fit all of them in this book (this time). A special thank-you needs to go out to my walk-on brothers: Grant Runnerstrum, Marc Preston, Rigo Diaz, Marc Raab, Paul Lewis, Eddy Chavez, Tom Sirotnak, Garrett Nolan, Jim Kortovich (Ohio State), and so many others. Together, we are proud graduates of ***Walk-On U***.

# The Walk-on U Editorial Team

## Judi K. Riefel

An avid football fan, Judi has more than 40 years in the allied healthcare field encompassing training as an RN, certification as a medical transcriptionist, medical staff coordinator, by the State of California Council for Private Postsecondary and Vocational Education. She has taught surgical and operating room procedures as well as anatomy, word processing, medical physiology, medical terminology, pharmacology, and medical transcription. She served as president of the California region of the Association for Healthcare Documentation Integrity (AHDI) and was a six-time president of the AHDI Orange County Chapter. She has received numerous regional awards and commendations from medical staffs countywide for her administrative work. Through her company, StarzMed, she currently provides medical editing and consulting services on HIPPA regulations to physicians nationwide. In addition, she volunteers her accomplished editing skills to premed university students. Her detail-oriented expertise enables her to provide out-of-the-box resolutions on many projects.

**Email: jr36781@gmail.com**

**Email: 0728starzmed0728@gmail.com**

## Dennis Fletcher

Dennis Fletcher's 50-year career in business communications, computers, marketing and management consulting has honed his writing skills. His connection to football came from his father, Johnny Flash Fletcher, who in 1935 was a starting quarterback for UCLA under Coach William Spaulding.

Dennis began his career at IBM and began teaching computer programming at night to students at Long Beach City College. He wrote the first college textbooks ever published on IBM's new RPG programming language and followed that with the first self-study audio course on RPG and a similar course on systems design and analysis.

In the field of communications, Dennis recently was involved in launching both the client newsletter and blog for IBM Business Partner Key Information Systems. In the nineties, Dennis authored a column on computer storage for *Database Trends* magazine called *The State of Storage*. He later authored a Web-based column for job-seekers called *Career Place* published by *Enterprise Systems Journal***.** In the eighties, he produced marketing support publications for Informatics, Inc., and he was publisher of his own IBM System/3X newsletter for L.A. area midrange computer users. At the same time, he wrote for *Systems Solutions*, a midrange magazine aimed at the IBM iSeries reseller channel, and for both

*News/400* and *Midrange Computing* magazines. Dennis continues to write under contract for clients in the Southern California area.

**Website: www.FletcherMarketing.us**

**Email: dennis@FletcherMarketing.us**

**Facebook: www.facebook.com/dennis.fletcher.1671**

**LinkedIn: Dennis A Fletcher**

**Fletcher Marketing Services**

**Chris Smith**

Chris Smith is an author, editor, and consultant specializing in the high-tech industry. He currently serves as Editorial Director of CC Communications, a high tech communications and public relations firm in La Verne, Calif., and as Editor of Key INsights, the corporate newsletter of Key Information Systems, an IBM systems integrator. With a bachelor's from the University of California at Berkeley, where he majored in English and minored in Journalism, and a master's in Journalism from the University of Colorado, Boulder, Chris later studied computer programming and AS/400 operations at Long Beach City College. A skier and football player in high school, Chris caught a few passes in his day playing tight end for the New Hampton School for Boys team in New Hampton, N.H. An award-winning writer with two Maggie Awards, four business books, and a collection of poetry to his credit, Chris began his newspaper career as a reporter in northern California, later worked as night city editor for the Rocky Mountain News in Denver. He was Communications Manager for McDonnell Douglas Corp. in Long Beach, Calif., and more recently worked as an editor for MC Press Online, where he edited the news and authored more than 300 articles on a broad range of high-tech topics.

**Website: www.cccommunicactionsonline.com**

**Email: chriswriting@cs.com**

**Facebook: Christopher Smith**

**La Verne, CA • Bridgehampton, NY**

**LinkedIn: Chris Smith**

**Editorial Director at CC Communications**